From HOMESTEADER to ART COLLECTOR

The Life and Times of Jacob Greenberg

ROBERT ZARETSKY

RODIN BOOKS™

Hardcover ISBN 978-1-957588-18-6
eBook ISBN 978-1-957588-19-3

PUBLISHED BY RODIN BOOKS INC
666 Old Country Road
Suite 510
Garden City, New York 11530

www.rodinbooks.com

Book and cover design by Alexia Garaventa

The Mechanic Arts High School photo courtesy of the Ramsey County Historical Society. The photo of the Oklahoma Clothing plant in Wewoka courtesy of Grady County Museum. Yearbook photo courtesy of the University of Minnesota Archives. All other photos were gladly provided by Joyce Greenberg.

Manufactured in the United States of America

RODIN
BOOKS

CONTENTS

PREFACE

In the fall of 2022, I received a message on my office phone at the University of Houston. In a crisp voice and business-like manner, the caller introduced herself as Joyce Greenberg. She had heard me speak several years before at the city's Jewish Community Center and now wondered if she could "pick my brain" on a pressing matter—namely, her late husband Jacob Greenberg. She wished to have someone write a book on Jacob, a remarkable man who "led an extraordinary life."

When I called Joyce back, she told me a good deal about Jacob's adventures and accomplishments. To be honest, I was impressed but also perplexed. I assured Joyce that while Jacob's life was undoubtedly extraordinary, I was undoubtedly the last person to write such a book. I had spent my professional life, after all, writing on modern French history, a field that had little to do with Jacob's life. Unfazed, Joyce insisted that I meet her for breakfast at Kenny & Ziggy's Delicatessen, then return to her apartment to tour her husband's art collection.

Two years and many bagels later, I am writing the preface to the book I was not qualified to write. It is a book unlike any book I have written. First, the story of Jacob Greenberg's life demands deeper knowledge than my own of not just American history but, more specifically, of the history of immigration of East European Jews to our shores in the late nineteenth century. Moreover, given the contours of Jacob's interests and professions, his biographer must also have a deeper grounding than I have in business and economic matters, as well as art and architectural history.

Most important, biographers need access to the personal papers and personal and official correspondence of their subjects. Similarly, they need archival sources that touch upon the life of their subjects. In the case of Jacob Greenberg, however, there was very little to be had on all these counts. Apart from a few stray letters, there appears to be no extant collection of personal papers or correspondence. Similarly, though I trawled various archives and contacted various institutions and corporations, the results were not as rewarding as I had hoped.

This leaves me with a confession and a conviction to share. First, I confess that my account of the life and times of Jacob Greenberg places greater emphasis on the exceptional times that span his life. Given the paucity of primary sources, I could hardly do otherwise. But I am also convinced the events and experiences that marked his century deeply marked Jacob Greenberg's life, helping to render it as exceptional as Joyce believes it was.

I need to express my gratitude to several individuals who have helped to guide my research. Professor Sandy Rikoon at the University of Missouri generously shared his research and insights into the Jewish homesteading movement during the last decades of the nineteenth century. In addition, Professor Tobias Brinkmann at Penn State University helped with potential archival sources for Jacob's time in Chicago, while Professor James Finck at the University of Arts and Sciences of Oklahoma did the same for Jacob's passage through Chickasha. Rabbi Donald Rossoff kindly shared both his memories of Jacob Greenberg and the eulogy he gave at his funeral. My sincere thanks as well to Pat Cunningham at the Grady County Museum, Rich Arpi at the Ramsey County Historical Society, Katelyn Morken at the University of Minnesota Archives, and Jocelyn Wilk at the Columbia University Archives for their help. And, of course, Arthur Klebanoff, the founder of Rodin Books, has been an insightful and invaluable partner in this undertaking.

Finally, I must thank Joyce Greenberg. Of course, were it not for her phone call, you would not be holding this book in your hands. I could not have written this book had it not been for Joyce's formidable character. I depended upon the many documents she cataloged over the years and the many books she collected on events and individuals that played roles in her husband's life. More important, though, I depended on her good humor and gentle persistence, her keen eye and kind gestures. While I hope I have made the case for Jacob Greenberg's exceptional life and character, I discovered that Joyce Greenberg's life and character are no less exceptional. I will always be grateful for this instance of *beshert* in my own life.

CHAPTER 1

A BADLANDS BEGINNING

There were no landmarks or lights. To lose your way on the prairie was like being lost at sea.

—RACHEL CALOF

I was amazed that my sophisticated husband was born on a homestead in North Dakota.

—JOYCE Z. GREENBERG

In the northeastern corner of North Dakota, roughly three miles east of the village of the well-named Starkweather, on a small patch of unfenced land under a boundless sky, huddles a handful of tombstones. Some are newly hewn from granite, and others are hammered from rusting tin, yet nearly all are over a century old. While this burial ground place is striking, it is hardly strange. Where else but on this sea of windswept wheat would one find the graves of eleven homesteaders who,

Jewish homesteader cemetery in Garske, North Dakota

in the tens of thousands, had flocked to the Dakotas in the late nineteenth and early twentieth centuries?

The British travel writer Jonathan Raban has described the power of these forgotten sites of memory in *Bad Land: An American Romance*, his sweeping account of the Dakotas. While driving across the prairie, he describes a moment when he stops near a cemetery. "Save for the odd empty jam jar, the individual graves were untended," Raban reports, "but someone kept the fences up and the grass neatly cut. . . . From the names in the graveyards, I thought I knew the people who had come out here: Europeans, mostly of my parents' generation, for whom belief in America, and its miraculous power of individual redemption, was the last great European religion. . . . Looking now at the fleet of lonely derelicts on the prairie, awash in grass and sinking fast, I could guess at how that faith had been shaken."[1]

Raban might just as well be describing the cemetery outside Starkweather. But he would have been surprised if he had read the names on the grave markers. Some of the inscriptions are too faded to read, but the others are carved not just in English but also in Hebrew. The family names of the dead, mostly children, are Jewish. Joseph Canter (1905–1918) and Anna Canter (1902–1914), Mandel Hill (1860–1935), and Joseph Adelman (died in 1907). Like Raban, one can only try to imagine how they lived and died.

But our imagination is not unaided in the cases of Israel Greenberg (1892–1903) and Charlotte Greenberg (1902–1906), whose names and dates are inscribed in polished granite. They were the children of Philip and Mollie Greenberg, whose nine other offspring survived. Paradoxically, the youngest, Jacob Greenberg, was also a middle child of sorts, born between the deaths of Israel and Charlotte in 1904. Yet not only did he survive, but he lived a long and exemplary life, one whose beginnings are rooted in this strange land that became home to strangers whose faith in the last of religions, American exceptionalism, and their faith in the first of the monotheistic religions, Judaism, were also shaken but rarely shattered.

The statistics still stagger—between 1881 and 1914, more than two million East European Jews arrived in the United States. Though several ports along the Eastern Seaboard, and eventually the port of Galveston, Texas, welcomed many of these ships, most passed by the Statue of Liberty and unloaded their passengers at the imposing immigration station on Ellis Island, which opened for business in 1892. More than 1.5 million immigrants who exited the other side went no further than the sprawling city across the narrow strait of water.

In effect, New York City *was* America for most Jewish immigrants—an image reinforced by countless memoirs and movies. Yet, while New York occupies center stage in the Jewish immigrant experience, it was not the only stage. New York was not America for those who, landing at Ellis Island, continued their journey farther west by rail, fueling the meteoric growth of Chicago or the twin cities of Minneapolis and St. Paul, while others reached California at the very moment the western frontier, as the historian Frederick Jackson Turner famously announced in 1893, was closing.

Over the past few decades, professional and amateur historians have turned their attention to these slighter vectors of assimilation for East European Jewish immigrants. Yet, one route has mostly escaped their attention—a route so surprising that, in its way, it is as dizzying as the sheer number of immigrants who settled in New York City. It led not to the urban centers in the Midwest or Far West but to the truly Wild West, the mostly empty expanses of the northern plains, where urban centers were as rare as mild winters. These harsh and seemingly endless lands, the native Dakotan Kathleen Norris observes, "often act as a crucible for those who inhabit them. Like Jacob's angel, the region requires that you wrestle with it before it bestows its blessing."[2]

The biblical reference holds special significance for the Jewish families who, with little means and less English, quit the Pale of Settlement—the vast stretch of territory, created in the eighteenth century by Czarist Russia, whose changing borders extended from the Baltic to the Black Sea—to resettle in the

Dakotas. Their reasons were several. In the last decades of the nineteenth century, the pogroms that swept the Pale posed a mortal threat to the Jews who had been banished there a century earlier. Importantly, however, recent research has revised the earlier portrayal of this era as one of unrelenting violence unleashed by Czarist authorities against a passive Jewish population. The depiction is now more nuanced and shaded. Led by the pathbreaking work of John Klier, historians now argue that local and national authorities tried to quell the explosions of anti-Semitism while determined Jewish villagers often tried to defend their *shtetls*, or villages, from ransacking peasants. Moreover, while the rise of violence was a crucial driver to immigration, so too were socio-economic factors, from the dim prospects for a future in the Old World of the shtetl and the bright promise of emancipation in the New World.[3]

Little in the lives of the thousands of East European Jews suggested, upon finding their feet in New York, they would soon find their way to North Dakota as homesteaders. Jews in southern Ukraine did launch a movement, Am Olam (Eternal People), to establish agricultural communities in America, but its reach was limited, and its impact was short-lived.[4] This is hardly surprising. Prevented by laws from owning land in Czarist Russia, few Jews had the chance to learn farming skills. Instead, most were traders or peddlers, wholly dependent on the commerce provided by close-knit communities nestled in urban ghettos or rural villages.

Not only did they lack the practical means to work the rocky soil of the high plains, but they lacked the conceptual means to even form an idea of such a life. Undoubtedly, it was easier to imagine the promised land of Israel than the badlands of America, to touch the stones of old Jerusalem than dig up the stones outside Starkweather. In her austere *Dakota Diaspora: Memoir of a Jewish Homesteader*, Sophie Trupin describes this sense of imaginative disconnect. Soon after landing in America with her family, Sophie began to hear the mysterious word. They were bound for *Nordokata*. It was there that "our traveling would come to an end. We had no idea what it would be like. But whatever it was, we would finally rest."[5]

In his classic work *Peasants into Frenchmen: The Modernization of Rural France, 1870–1914*, the historian Eugen Weber traces the fledgling Third Republic's response to France's humiliating defeat in the Franco-Prussian War of 1870. To build a republic capable of rivaling the German Reich, officials first had to lay a solid foundation: a citizenry formed by common traditions, values, and even language. This was a formidable task in a country where most citizens did not speak French. Instead, France was a patchwork of peoples who spoke several distinct languages—from Provençal, Breton, and Flemish to Corsican, Alsatian, and Basque—along with hundreds of patois, or dialects. Parisian inspectors who toured the provinces found an alarming state of affairs—Frenchmen and women unable to speak French and unwilling to surrender the old ways of their community for the new ways of the republic. The task at hand was to forge a citizenry from a population viewed as "backward, savage, barbarous, wild, living like beasts."[6]

Across the Atlantic, American immigration officials faced a similar challenge. They, too, confronted millions of men, women, and children unfamiliar with the nation's language and ways. But there were two crucial differences. Whereas France's task was to transform those already deeply rooted in French soil into French citizens, America's task was to make Americans of those who had just arrived. In the case of East European Jewish immigrants, though, there was a fascinating wrinkle. Rather than France's effort to make peasants into Frenchmen by inculcating a love for the abstract notion of a nation, Jewish immigrants, most of who had no ties to the land in Russia or the Pale of Settlement, were to be made Americans by rooting them in the soil of the nation. In brief, to become American, these one-time town and urban dwellers had to *become* peasants.

This, at least, was the conviction of several key Jewish philanthropic agencies: the Jewish Agriculturalists' Aid Society (JAAS), based in Chicago, and the Hebrew Emigrant Aid Society (HEAS) and the Jewish Agricultural and Industrial Aid Society (JAIAS), both headquartered in New York. Their common goal was to Americanize the great waves of Jewish immigrants arriving on our shores by, quite literally, farming them out to rural America. Staffed largely by a de facto aristocracy of German-American Jews, the agencies feared the impact this massive influx of their East European brethren—so very different in aspect and language—would have on the public.

If the observations of the waspish novelist Henry James, having just returned to New York from London, were any indication, the impact would be disastrous. Touring lower Manhattan, James was shocked by its changed character. "There is no swarming like that of Israel when once Israel has got a start, and the scene here bristled, at every step, with the signs and sounds, immitigable, unmistakable, of a Jewry that had burst all bounds." What he described as "the gathered past of Israel pushing through" foretold, in his eyes, the "Hebrew conquest of New York."[7] Though on the opposite side of the political and ideological divide, the social reformer Jacob Riis nevertheless echoed, if not adhered to, James's racist stereotypes. In 1890, he published *How the Other Half Lives*, a detailed and devastating account of the tenements of New York City. One of the chapters, titled "Jewtown," captures both the powerful and problematic nature of Riis's approach.

> No need of asking here where we are. The jargon of the street, the signs of the sidewalk, the manner and dress of the people, their unmistakable physiognomy betray their race at every step. . . . Thrift is the watchword of Jewtown, as of its people the world over. It is at once its strength and its fatal weakness, its cardinal virtue and its foul disgrace. Become an over-mastering passion with these people who come here in droves from Eastern Europe to escape persecution, from which freedom could be bought only with gold, it has enslaved them in bondage worse than that from which they fled. Money is their God.

The "thrift" of these Jewish immigrants, continues Riis, thrives in the dark and destitute streets of lower Manhattan.

> Penury and poverty are wedded everywhere to dirt and disease, and Jewtown is no exception. It could not well be otherwise in such crowds, considering especially their low intellectual

> status. . . . Typhus fever and smallpox are bred here . . . they sprout naturally among the hordes that bring the germs with them from across the sea, and whose first instinct is to hide their sick lest the authorities carry them off to the hospital to be slaughtered, as they firmly believe.[8]

German-American Jews were torn between the dire plight of their fellow Jews, fleeing persecution at home, and the fear that their arrival, so sudden and unsettling, would spark the same hatreds that made them leave Germany. In fact, these new immigrants also struck many in the American Jewish community as strange and discomforting. So much so that, at times, they rallied to propose limitations on the number of immigrants and even paid for return tickets to Europe for hundreds of Jewish men who were unable to support themselves in New York. As Augustus Levy, the HEAS's secretary, confessed, "The mode of life of these people in Russia has stamped upon them the ineffaceable marks of permanent pauperism, only disgrace and a lowering of the opinion in which American Israelites are held by this community can result from the continued residence among us of such an addition to the Jewish population. Every crime against property or the person committed by one of these wretches will throw obloquy over our race throughout the land."[9]

Yet, many prominent Jews were determined, for moral as well as political reasons, to welcome their coreligionists. The question was how best to assimilate the thousands of men, women, and children arriving daily in New York Harbor from distant urban ghettos and rural shtetls. Not only was the question thorny, but it was also pressing. In a report published just one year before Riis's book, United Hebrew Charities sounded a warning. Referring to a rash of sensationalist stories in local papers, it declared that while Jewish overcrowding in New York City's Lower East Side "has too often been the subject of extravagant word-painting in the daily press, any passer-by cannot be blind to the fact that the good name of New York Judaism is endangered unless remedial measures are promptly devised to correct the evil . . . of this unlawful and farspreading [*sic*] feature of our tenement system." The *New York Times* echoed this concern, warning that the great influx of East European Jews would "appreciably swell the ranks of our beggars, ragpickers, organ grinders, low criminals, and other objectionable classes."[10]

What, though, could be done? The population density of lower Manhattan, especially its east side, hovered near critical mass. "It is said," Riis noted, "that nowhere in the world are so many people crowded together on a square mile than here."[11] Demographic studies have since confirmed Riis's remark. In 1900, the density of the Tenth Ward—home to the Jewish immigrants from East Europe—outstripped that of any other city in the world. As many as 1,100 people were crowded onto an acre thick with squalid four- or five-story tenements. As one recent study has observed, the word *density* became so attached to the Tenth Ward that urban architects tended to shun it.[12]

For Jewish immigrant agencies in New York, an obvious first step was to divert newly arriving immigrants to other cities, either on the East Coast or inland as far as Chicago. While this lessened the pressure on New York, the effort to disperse Jewtown risked creating Jewtowns in other cities. Whether in New York or Chicago, immigrant Jews would only confirm the stereotype of the Jew as an uprooted alien who can thrive only in an urban setting, a place where he can ply his one skill: a trader of commodities or currency. In 1890, the German-Jewish paper *The American Israelite* reported that resettling the "persecuted, down-trodden and degenerated Hebrews" on American soil would prevent an "increase of Nihilism, Socialism, Communism and such other extravagances to which people just escaping the bonds of slavery are most prone." "In a couple of generations," the editor predicted, working the land would "restore the race to its pristine character."[13]

Thomas Jefferson might well have agreed. In his *Notes on the State of Virginia*, he affirmed his belief in the redemptive and peculiarly American quality of tilling the land. "Those who labour in the earth are the chosen people of God, if ever he had a chosen people, whose breasts he has made his peculiar deposit for substantial and genuine virtue. It is the focus in which he keeps alive that sacred fire which otherwise might escape from the face of the earth."[14] While he was referring to American farmers, not biblical cultivators, Jefferson's claim would have found a ready audience among American Jews. How better to assimilate their coreligionists from the shtetls and ghettos of Eastern Europe than by farming them out to the American heartland?

Baron Maurice de Hirsch shared this belief. By the 1880s, the German-Jewish entrepreneur, who made his fame and fortune with the building of the Constantinople–Vienna railway, had turned his eyes from the Near East to East Europe. In fact, the opening of the rail line opened Hirsch's eyes to the abject conditions of the Jewish communities in the Ottoman Empire.[15]

With the death of their only child in 1887, Hirsch and his wife decided to invest their staggering wealth—estimated to be more than $1 billion—in Jewish immigration projects equally staggering in their nature and numbers. "I have lost my son," he wrote to a friend, "but not my heir. Humanity is now my heir."[16]

Though these heirs included Christians and Muslims, Hirsch channeled most of his charity to Eastern and Russian Jews. But he was a source not just of financial but also inspirational capital. Rather than infusing his wealth into existing organizations, Hirsch invented organizations to manage projects that, in his words, "might appear fantastic at first glance."[17] Hirsch had but one message for his coreligionists: Go west. He insisted the future of his fellow Jews lay in foreign lands in North and South America where they could begin new lives. In 1889, he established the Maurice de Hirsch Fund to facilitate the immigration of Russian Jews to the United States. Two years later, in an era when colonization was still portrayed, if only by the colonizer, as a noble pursuit, Hirsch founded the Jewish Colonization Association (JCA). Based in London, the JCA's mission was, in Hirsch's words, "to give a portion of my companions in faith the possibility of finding a new existence, primarily as farmers . . . in those lands where the laws and religious tolerance permit them to carry on the struggle for existence."[18]

In effect, Hirsch plowed part of his fortune into furnishing plows to Jews. While his contemporary, Theodor Herzl, argued that European Jewry could be free only by embracing their Jewish identity in a Jewish state, Hirsch insisted they could be fully free only by shedding their Jewish faith and settling in a secular state. As his biographer Matthias Lehmann observes,

Hirsch "professed on many occasions that assimilation and intermarriage were the future of the Jews, and the only way to overcome the so-called Jewish question."[19] A thoroughly secular Jew, Hirsch was unsentimental about the faith of his ancestors, considering it a burden to relinquish, not a birthright to retain. In an interview with the *New York Herald* in 1889, he was blunt: "The Jewish question can only be solved by the disappearance of the Jewish race."[20]

Where better to disappear than the southern pampas of Argentina, a sparsely populated nation eager to grow, or the northern prairies of the fledging states of the Dakotas, equally keen to populate the land? By forsaking their homes in the Old World and founding settlements in the wild places of the New World, these Jewish pioneers, in turn, would be reborn. Shouldering the task of midwife, the JCA and Hirsch Fund both supported existing Jewish immigrant agencies and created new ones in the United States to bring over and, when possible, spread out Eastern European Jews. In 1900, the fund created the JAIAS. Like the floundering JAAS, founded by Rabbi Abraham Levy, the JAIAS's raison d'être was to assist Jewish immigrants in putting down their roots not in Lower Manhattan but in the upper plains. Lastly, in 1901, the sudden and massive influx of Romanian Jews, spurred by anti-Semitic legislation by their government, also led to the creation of the awkwardly named Industrial Removal Office (IRO).

For these agencies, it was a choice of last resort to keep immigrants in New York, Chicago, or any other city. Doing so, they feared, would undo the security of American Jews by conjuring the very same threat—anti-Semitic violence—that had driven their coreligionists from their homes in Europe.

They were driven by the belief, frequently repeated by the IRO's general manager, David Bessler, that they were helping these newcomers find "their own salvation."[21] The IRO, along with the JAIAS, shared the JAAS sense of mission: "We take the unfortunate out of the overcrowded and sickly ghetto, from the midst of misery and squalor, out into the country where the air is pure and healthful; we change their occupation from a peddler, or laborer, or a tailor . . . into the honorable position of farmer."[22] Echoing this language, the JAAS sent about 350 recent immigrants, gathered in nearly eighty different groups, to escape "the enslaving sweatshop or unpromising and degrading 'peddling' in the city and start out as farmers."[23]

While the earlier and sporadic attempts to alchemize Jewish peddlers into American farmers were communalist—inspired, in part, by the Am Olam movement—the JAAS and JAIAS emphasized individual farms. No doubt inspired by his own family's history as landowners, Hirsch believed that "the Jews have not lost the agricultural qualities that their forefathers possessed." But they would be independent farmers, he insisted. According to the JAIAS leadership, communal farms were impractical, "merely transferring Jewish Ghettos from large cities to agricultural districts."[24] Similarly, Levy insisted on the Jeffersonian ideal of the independent farmer. The "application of *individualism*," he affirmed, "has proven to be as essential to the success of the undertaking . . . of the would-be Jewish farmer."[25]

What was proved, instead, was the unwitting prescience of Levy's phrase *would-be farmer*. Having lent over $100,000 to Jewish immigrants who were as unacquainted with agriculture as they were with English, the JAAS, undone by unpaid loans and unwilling investors, shuttered its windows in 1910.[26] The JAIAS proved more resilient by making better use of the Homestead Act and by making better farmers through the visits of agricultural experts. In 1911, the organization reported that they had helped to settle about five thousand Jewish immigrants on farms, a number that by 1927 had ballooned to eighty thousand in rural communities across the country.[27] Though a fraction of the Jewish American population of four million, it remains an astonishing number and includes the approximately eight thousand East European Jews who were planted on the soil of North Dakota during the closing decades of the nineteenth century. While most of these accidental pioneers did not remain long enough for their roots to dig deep, their confrontation with a physical climate as hostile as the political climate they had fled makes for one of the most surprising facets of the Jewish immigrant experience in the United States.

In 1882, the first wave of Jewish immigrants settled on a partly forested tract of land several miles north of Bismarck. Called Painted Woods after the name of the closest village, the settlement was the brainchild of Judah Wechsler. Recently arrived as a rabbi in St. Paul, the German-born Wechsler was the driving force behind this utopian scheme for a Jewish settlement in the northern plains. Convinced that the future of American Jewry would be reformed or would not be at all, Wechsler was disturbed by the orthodox practices of the Russian Jews and determined to make them model American Jews. He was also disturbed that the dramatic influx of Jewish immigrants in St. Paul was raw meat for anti-Semitic demagogues to toss to the crowds. With a sense of urgency, Wechsler declared that the immigrants "are our kindred and it is our duty to elevate them to a higher place to become good citizens of this country."[28]

And so, Wechsler looked north for a solution. Given the ease of obtaining land grants in North Dakota, resettling the newcomers from the Russian Pale to the Dakotan plains would not only ease demographic pressures in St. Paul but also ease the transition of these peddlers into farmers. Driven by this sense of mission, Wechsler tirelessly raised money from skeptical groups and individuals, including his own congregation in St. Paul, to make the settlement a going concern. At first, his efforts were rewarded. From 1882 to 1885, the colony quadrupled in size, from an initial dozen families in 1882 to fifty Russian and Romanian families in 1885. By then, the colony boasted large herds of cows and oxen and tilled more than 1,400 acres of land. But the experiment was short-lived when a series of unusually harsh winters, dry summers, and a prairie fire proved too great a blow for the fledgling farmers. By 1886, unable to persuade his congregants to continue their support of the settlement now on life support, Wechsler quit his rabbinical position for a new post in Meridian, Alabama, and the settlers quit Painted Woods for nearby cities in neighboring states. All that is left of their presence is a school district named Montefiore, named after the Jewish philanthropist Sir Moses Montefiore, whom the settlers, including Jacob Greenberg's father, Philip Greenberg, had approached for the purchase of a Torah.[29]

Nevertheless, new waves of immigrants continued to spill into North Dakota. As early as 1882, roughly two dozen Russian Jews, with the help of the HEAS, purchased homesteads near the village of Garske in Ramsey County. After two years of punishing weather and failed crops, the unprepared and overwhelmed settlers—described in one report as "inexperienced, thoughtless and very poor"—left their homesteads for other settlements or towns.[30] Whereas the Painted Woods settlers left behind just one name—Montefiore—the Garske settlers left behind several names engraved on tombstones in the abandoned cemetery. As for the houses that, lacking the means to buy lumber, they built with sod, they slowly subsided into the same soil they had been scraped from.

The lifespan of other settlements, however, proved slightly more resilient. Near the town of Devils Lake, the number of Jewish homesteads quadrupled, growing from ten to more than forty by 1889. The community had, in fact, grown large enough to merit its own post office that the settlers named Benzion. The name for the post office was no doubt proposed by its first (and last) postmaster, Benyomen (or Benjamin) Greenberg—Philip's brother and Jacob's future uncle—who cast the settlement as a new Zion. At first, these hopes did not seem utterly utopian. By the end of the decade, the settlers were cultivating about 3,500 acres of wheat and flax fields.[31] Yet the crop yield was not enough to cover the bills, much less pay back earlier loans, often tied to high interest rates, from Jewish organizations based in the Twin Cities. But the occasional infusion of cash to service the loans, intermittent arrival of new immigrants, and the sheer persistence of the earlier settlers kept the Devils Lake settlement alive and, at times, kicking. In 1901, in fact, Philip Greenberg declared that thanks to a new threshing machine, it was "the first time that the crop of the Jewish farmers has been threshed in good season."[32] Three years later, Greenberg would announce yet more good news: the birth of his son Jacob.

By the time of Jacob's birth, the Greenberg clan had become the aristocracy of the Devils Lake settlement. In the company of his wife Mollie Greenberg (née Grawoig) and their other children—Herman, Samuel, and Bessie—Philip Greenberg had arrived in this northeastern corner of the Great Plains in 1887. The distance between the plains of North Dakota and the steppes of Bessarabia, Philip's birthplace, was not as great as it might seem. Both regions, swept by grassland prairies, had been recently absorbed by powerful neighbors—America and Russia—and were home to several ethnic and religious communities. Before winning statehood in 1889, North Dakota had become a magnet for Norwegians, Swedes, Irish, Germans, Moravians, and Jews. The latter's numbers—roughly eight thousand—formed 7.5 percent of the total population of 190,000 in the 1890 census. Similarly, Bessarabia had long been a crossroads for a multitude of peoples, principally Bulgarians, Greeks, Russians, Moldovans, and Armenians. The Jewish inhabitants bulked large, constituting more than 10 percent of the area's population by the end of the nineteenth century.[33]

Along with his brothers Benjamin and Jacob, Philip was born in the regional capital of Kishinev (present-day Chisiau) in 1861 to Abraham and Bessie Greenberg. The size of the city's Jewish community ballooned during the second half of the century, from slightly more than ten thousand to more than fifty thousand in 1897.[34] While a small number formed part of a commercial and industrial elite whose success attracted Jews from other parts of Bessarabia, most Jews lived lives of quiet desperation. This seems to have been true for the Greenbergs.

While the one existing account of the family history suggests they quit Kishinev for the United States because their sons had become old enough for the Russian military draft, material scarcity almost surely played a role as well. Nevertheless, the prospect of losing his sons to the Russian army was, no doubt, the immediate cause of the Greenbergs' decision to leave the Pale.

It was thus in 1879—two years before the entire region erupted in bloody pogroms—that Abraham and Amelia Greenberg—by then, Abraham had remarried following the death of Bessie—quit Kishinev, reached Amsterdam, and embarked in the steerage of a Greek ship bound for the United States. Though they disembarked at Ellis Island, the Greenbergs did not, as did most of their fellow Jewish immigrants, remain in lower Manhattan. Instead, they headed west to Traverse City, a growing town connected to two railways in northern Michigan. It was here that Abraham's sister, with the married name of Nettleman, had already settled. The Nettlemans already had more than enough company to make a minyan. In fact, the town's Jewish community was large enough to fund the building of a synagogue, Temple Beth El, in 1884, whose doors have never since closed.[35]

By the time the doors opened in 1886, however, the Greenbergs were no longer there to walk through them. That same year, Abraham and Amelia moved again. Making his living by peddling—perhaps the same profession he plied in Kishinev—Abraham was undoubtedly seeking a more stable and stationary livelihood. Hence, the appeal of the Homestead Act of 1862, which he probably learned about from fellow peddlers or customers. In 1879, the act was extended to the territory

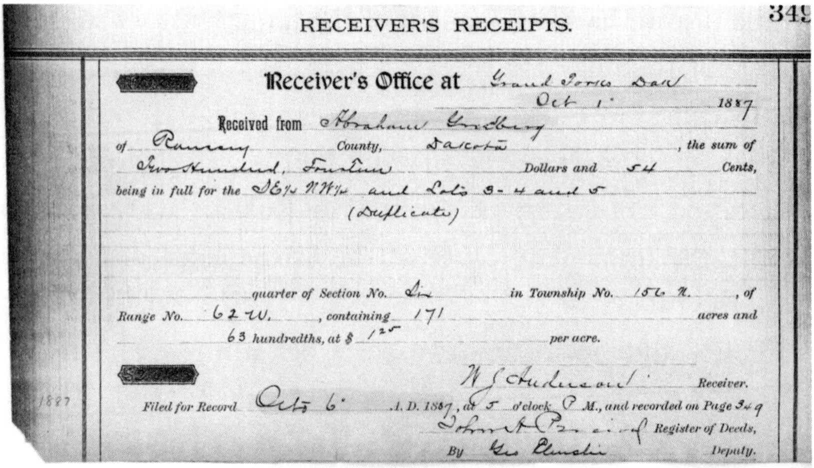

RECEIVER'S RECEIPTS. 349

Receiver's Office at Grand Forks Dak
Oct 1 1887

Received from Abraham Greenberg
of Ramsey County, Dakota, the sum of
Two Hundred, Fourteen Dollars and 54 Cents,
being in full for the SE¼ NW¼ and Lots 3-4 and 5
(Duplicate)
quarter of Section No. Six in Township No. 156 N., of
Range No. 62 W., containing 171 acres and
63 hundredths, at $ 1.25 per acre.

W J Anderson Receiver.

Filed for Record Oct 6 A. D. 1887, at 5 o'clock P M., and recorded on Page 349
[illegible] Register of Deeds,
By [illegible] Deputy.

The 1887 homestead deed signed by Abraham Greenberg

of North Dakota, offering 160 acres of land in exchange for the commitment to work those acres for five consecutive years. It was an offer too good to refuse for the desperate and the dreamers. By 1886, when Abraham and Amelia filed for a lot in Ramsey County, more than one hundred thousand fellow homesteaders had already preceded them to North Dakota. Convinced of the soundness of the investment, Abraham doubled down the following year, paying $214.57 on October 1 for three more lots so that his sons and families could join him.[36] This purchase, seemingly prosaic, was quietly historic: From peddlers in Eastern Europe, the Greenbergs had turned themselves into pioneers in Western America.

In 1978, Devera Stocker, a researcher at the Jewish Historical Society of Michigan who was writing about Jewish immigrants in Traverse City at the turn of the twentieth century, contacted Nettie Greenberg Epstein. The researcher had found records of the Greenberg family's brief sojourn in the city and a donation they made to synagogue and hoped to learn more about Philip and Mollie from their surviving children. It was only several months after Stocker had sent her letter that the eighty-year-old Nettie replied. Noting that she found the researcher's query of "great interest," Nettie offered a telling explanation for her belated reply. "As I think back, it seems we were not very curious about the early life of our parents, either in Russia or the U.S.A. The subject never came up or was discussed."[37]

Perhaps it is not surprising, then, that when the same researcher reached out with the same request to Nettie's brother Jacob, he never bothered to answer. His second wife, Joyce Greenberg, recalls that Jacob spent little time thinking back. Instead, like so many other children of that generation of Jewish immigrants, he preferred to think forward. One practical consequence of this lack of curiosity "about the early life of their parents"—which included their years in North Dakota—is a paucity of primary source material.

This scarcity of material is also, in a sense, structural. Jewish farmers, as a rule, spent only a few years on their homesteads before moving, for family or financial reasons, into towns or cities. As a result, not only did they lack time, energy, and resources to record their experiences while they homesteaded, but once they left the land, there seemed little reason to recall those earlier experiences. As a result, the historians Norton Stern and William Kramer discovered during their own effort to collect primary documents on this subject that "little material survives in terms of Jewish agricultural continuity in North Dakota."[38]

Yet, we are not entirely dependent on Nettie Epstein's account, along with occasional references to the family in contemporary documents. There are two other remarkable sources that capture the contours, if not the full texture, of Jacob's early life in South Dakota: *Rachel Calof's Story: Jewish Homesteader on the Northern Plains* and Sophie Trupin's *Dakota Diaspora: Memoirs of a Jewish Homesteader*. J. Sanford Rikoon, a historian at the University of Missouri, discovered Calof's account while doing research at the American Jewish Archives in Cincinnati. Her manuscript, framed by Rikoon's meticulous scholarship, was published in 1995 by Indiana University Press. While Calof wrote in Yiddish and did not write with an eye on publication, Trupin wrote in English and most certainly wrote to be read. Her goal was to remind readers that not all Jewish immigrants were city dwellers.[39]

Inevitably, Calof and Trupin's experiences differ in many ways, not just from the Greenbergs but also from one another. Yet, they also often align in telling ways. Born in Russia in 1876, Rachel Bella Kahn arrived in the United States in 1894 as an eighteen-year-old mail-order bride. Her fiancé, Abraham Calof, met her at Ellis Island, but they did not remain long in New York. Abraham had already made plans for the two of them to join the rest of his family, who had gone to North Dakota three months earlier to become homesteaders. We can only make something of ourselves, he explained to his bride, if we "avail ourselves of the offer of free land." Rachel agreed: "It seemed a godsend to penniless people who could not hope to buy land."[40] Sophie Trupin also arrived in the United States without a father. In 1904, her father, Harry Turnoy, left his wife, Gittel, and children in Russia. His goal was to make a new life in the New World, then send for his family. Four years later, in 1908, they joined him in that "place called 'Nordokota.'"[41]

In 1887, Philip Greenberg was living in Petoskey, Michigan, with his wife Mollie Grawoig—whose family had emigrated from the northern Ukraine city of Berdichev—and their three children, Herman, Sam, and Bessie. Philip supported the family as a customer peddler, selling merchandise to farmers he visited in his horse and buggy. This familiarity with farming, and the prospect of working rather than wandering across the land, undoubtedly led Philip to homestead alongside his father in North Dakota.

What was Mollie's reaction when she first saw her new home, which was most probably still a sod house? Having lived in rural Petoskey and perhaps having been prepared by Philip, she was probably not as surprised, much less as stunned, as were Rachel Calof and Gittel Turnoy. The former discovered, upon arriving at her homestead, that she and Abraham would live with his parents until a roof could be put on their "wood shanty." Her first impression of its interior proved indelible: "As we entered my heart turned to ice at what greeted the eyes. This was my first sight of what awaited me as a pioneer woman. The furniture consisted of a bed, a rough table made of wood slats, and two benches. The house was divided up into two sections, the other being the kitchen which held a stove and beside it a heap of dried cow dung. When I inquired about this, I was told that this was the only fuel this household had. They had no firewood at all."[42]

Gittel Turnoy's reaction to the sight of the shanty—for which she and her children had followed Harry Turnoy across two continents and an ocean—largely reenacts Rachel Calof's first glimpse of the "dismal spectacle" of her new home. "When my mother finally arrived," writes Sophie Trupin, "she was dismayed and horrified at what she found. She saw a sod house with a rough, splintered floor, a crude homemade table with two benches which my father had fashioned from planks, iron bedsteads with sagging springs, and a blackened kitchen range. The well was in the valley at the foot of the hill upon which our house stood."[43] We do not know the details of the house where the Greenbergs first settled, but it must have fallen somewhere between the "dismal" and the "crude," between a flimsy shanty with dirt floors and a sod cabin with wood floors. The distance between their new home and the homes they had left behind in Petoskey or Traverse City—or, indeed, Kishinev or Berdichev—must have been disorienting. These settlers had escaped the densely populated world of the ghetto, webbed by shared religious and cultural traditions and wracked by spasms of anti-Semitic violence, for a world free not just of anti-Semitism but free of most everything else—from floors to roofs, from community to solidarity—they had associated with normal life. For the Greenbergs, this brave new world must have resembled the one that greeted Gittel Turnoy: "An alien, heathen land, harsh and bare and hostile."[44]

A tragic irony runs through the living conditions of these Jewish immigrants. The Turnoys, Calofs, and Greenbergs, drawn by the promise of free land, had made their own way to North Dakota. Yet, many of their fellow would-be farmers found their way to the northern plains with the aid and advice of Jewish charities like the Hirsch Fund and agencies like the JAIAS. Their goal was to disperse the ghetto by diverting (and ultimately draining) Jewish immigrants from the suffocating density of urban centers and jump-starting their Americanization by seeding them in the heartland. At first, though, these pioneers of the American West found themselves living in the same cramped and claustrophobic conditions as their urban brethren. Though the Calof's shanty stood alone in endless and empty fields, its inhabitants lived on top of one another—at times, quite literally—within its twelve-by-fourteen-foot dimensions. The leitmotif that weaves through Calofs' memoir is the lack of privacy imposed by "the terrible crowding of many people into a small space." Of the many burdens she bore, Calof insists this was the greatest one of all.[45]

The Greenbergs seemed determined to create the same density inside their little shack on the prairie, if only by adding children to their family. Mollie would undoubtedly have agreed with Rachel Calof's dry observation that the "most dependable state of affairs I knew during the many years I lived on the prairie was pregnancy."[46] (An observation as tragic as it is limpid: Calof reveals that her "torn insides,"[47] despite repeated operations, never fully recovered from her nine deliveries.) Along with the three children they brought to the Garske homestead, the Greenbergs added eight more in rapid succession: Myron (b. 1889), Israel (b. 1892), Ethel (b. 1894), Morris (b. 1896), Charles (b. 1899), Nettie (b. 1900), Charlotte (b. 1902), and finally Jacob (b. 1904). As the grave markers in the nearby cemetery remind us, two of the siblings—Israel and Charlotte—died in childhood, but the house nevertheless teemed with Greenbergs until 1906 when they rented out the farm and moved to Devils Lake.

There were yet other material conditions on the great plains that paralleled those in the great cities. The prairie dwellings, like many city tenements, lacked indoor plumbing. The Trupins trekked to the well dug at the foot of the hill upon which their house stood, while the Calofs would move their shanty to accompany the wells they had to dig. Heating during the winter was also a dicey affair in both the urban and rural settings; in both cases, families often depended on the heat generated by bodies piled near one another to survive cold nights. Even the intensity of labor was similar in both worlds. Many immigrants trapped in the infamous sweatshops of New York's Lower East Side were also forced to work fifteen-hour days (and nights), not unlike the unrelenting labor of the men who tilled the soil of the Dakotan soil. "It seems to me as I look back," Sophie Trupin writes, "all the rows and heaps of rocks that lay along each cleared field were stained with the sweat of these zealots."[48]

There were yet other similarities—from the threat of asphyxiation from smoking stoves to the threat of fire sweeping through a sweatshop or a wheat field—but there were even more important differences. On the streets of Manhattan's Lower East Side and the Maxwell Street neighborhood in Chicago, one could not help but breathe Yiddishkeit. The language, culture, institutions, and practices of European Judaism were omnipresent. On the plains of North Dakota, however, being Jewish proved as arduous as being prosperous. Time and again, Calof recalls the challenges that Jewish law imposed on her family's struggle for survival. During their second and especially harsh winter on the homestead, the family, which had little else than wheat seed for nourishment, never butchered their cow or one of their oxen. The reason was simple: "I don't believe it ever occurred to anyone to kill or eat an animal that had not been ritually slaughtered according to the precepts of our religion."

At times, though, it proved more imperative to break than to keep kashrut. When Abraham had bought what he thought was a jar of pickled herring that was, instead, pickled pigs' knuckles, the Calofs kept both the secret and the jar. No less tellingly, when they prepared to mark the birth of a son, the Calofs sent for a traveling *shochet,* or kosher butcher, to slaughter an ox for the celebratory meal. Though the shochet discovered that the ox was *traif* (not kosher), he nevertheless ordered Rachel, weakened by her son's birth, to prepare the beef. According to Jewish law, he explained to his shocked but grateful wife, mothers were morally bound to maintain the health of their children, regardless of kosher law. Rather than seeking out a shochet, Harry Turnoy, who had learned so many other skills on the job, from tilling the soil to building a house, also learned to slaughter his animals according to Jewish law. He even had, Trupin notes, a special ritual knife for the purpose.

One can only wonder if the Greenbergs loosened the laws during the early days as homesteaders. They kept an Orthodox kosher home and, during the winter months, had kosher meat shipped to them from a rabbi, Benjamin Papermaster, who also served as the shochet to the Jewish community in Grand Forks. (The synagogue he founded and led for nearly half a century, Temple B'nai Israel, still stands in Grand Forks.) Moreover, as owners of the area's sole Torah, the Greenbergs hosted not just the annual holiday services but also a *shamash,* or synagogue sexton, Sam Yaffe, who traveled from St. Paul for the occasions. "The only time we ate meat during the summer," recalled Nettie Epstein, "was when the shochet happened to come to the area for some special occasion. He then came to our farm to do some slaughtering." (In her letter to Devora Stocker, Nettie Greenberg Epstein spells *shamash* as "shamus." Humphrey Bogart fans will recall that in *The Big Sleep,* his character Philip Marlowe refers to himself as a "shamus," which, by the 1930s, had come to mean "private investigator" in American slang.)

Born in 1900, however, Nettie's memories do not reach back to the first decade of the family's experiences on the farm. This was the time before Philip added rooms to the house, had a series of successful harvests, and had the honor of becoming the superintendent of the one-room schoolhouse that stood not too far from their own home. The period stretching from 1897—when Philip Greenberg reported that, thanks to the new mechanized thresher, the community enjoyed a successful harvest—to 1907 marked the golden years for most Jewish homesteaders.

But the earlier years must have been as testing a time for the Greenbergs as for their fellow homesteaders. It was during this same period that Philip's brother Benjamin, perhaps in response to the strictures of kashrut, became a vegetarian. He also upheld civil law as the local justice of the peace and religious law by leading various holiday celebrations. There is no doubt what Benjamin would have done, say, with a jar of pigs' knuckles during those years. He had not one but two excellent reasons to leave the jar unopened. As for his brother Philip, perhaps just one excellent reason would have been enough. Or perhaps not.

What we do know is that in 1906, two years after Jacob was born, the Greenbergs moved out of their farmhouse and moved into a larger house in Devils Lake. The reason was that their children were growing up and reaching a critical age, one that had nothing to do with the military draft—Abraham and Amelia Greenberg's reason to flee Kishinev with their three sons—and everything to do with marriage. Since the neighboring farms had few Jewish candidates, Nettie recalled, "my parents worried that they might marry non-Jews."

Jacob Greenberg standing outside his childhood home in Devils Lake, North Dakota

From one continent and generation to another, the fears of these Jewish parents greatly changed. They were no longer kept awake at night by the prospect of losing their sons to the Russian army and anti-Semitism but instead by losing their sons (and daughters) to American culture and secularism. It was less a question of keeping the kids on the farm than keeping them Jewish. Ultimately, the parents could not satisfy both imperatives. To keep the kids Jewish, they could not keep the farm. This was one of the factors in the decline and fall of Jewish homesteads—a fall so steep that, by 1965, only three of more than forty-six thousand rural households in North Dakota had even a trace of Jewish ancestry. Sandy Rikoon notes that the average lifespan of a Jewish homestead was seven years. What better number for a people of the Torah? Seven was the number of days it took Yahweh to finish and rest from his cosmic experiment. Perhaps seven years was all the time needed for these few thousand Jewish pioneers to finish their earthly experiment.[49]

Yet, the Greenbergs stand apart. They worked and lived on the land for eighteen years, more than double the average land tenure. The depth and duration of Rachel and Abraham Calof's devotion to the soil were no less exceptional. They remained on the farm for more than two decades. Over the years, the Calofs had, like the Greenbergs, also expanded their farmhouse; like the Greenbergs, they had also become pillars of the community. What Rachel Calof recalled about her time on the prairie would have struck a deep chord with the Greenbergs: "We could look back with pride on our accomplishments. We had come as raw immigrants without resources or training to a stark wilderness in a strange county, and we tamed the land and made it fit for humans."[50] It was a stunning achievement of courage and commitment, persistence and intelligence—an achievement that must have influenced their children. Though Jacob was just three when the family left Devils Lake, his family's prairie years became part of his heritage and character.

CHAPTER 2

THE ST. PAUL YEARS

In 1922, Minneapolis Jewry enjoys the painful distinction of being the lowest esteemed community in the land so far as the non-Jewish population of the city is concerned.

–MAURICE LEFKOWITZ

In the pupils of Mechanic Arts High School of St. Paul, you find democracy exemplified. Here is a working model of the melting pot. Rich and poor, Jew and gentile, bourgeoisie, proletarian and aristocrat, are on one plane of equality.

–1919 MECHANIC ARTS HIGH SCHOOL STUDENT YEARBOOK

By the second half of the nineteenth century, the fledgling state of Minnesota began competing with other northwestern states and territories for new settlers. Local railroads built temporary housing for new arrivals drawn by the "fact admitting of no dispute" that Minnesota "contains more natural wealth within her borders than any other area of corresponding size on the face of the earth." Not to be outdone in grandiose claims, the state's immigration board published a broadsheet addressed to "Laboring Men . . . Landless men . . . All Men," promising them a home of "unparalleled opportunities and matchless resources" that would transform immigrants, making them "physically and mentally stronger, purer, and nobler."[1]

Presenting itself as a land of promise, one whose "lofty hills, graceful slopes, verdant nooks, crystal streams, and limpid lakes" bordered on the Edenic, Minnesota drew several hundred German Jews in the 1850s and 1860s. For many, the decision to leave Germany was made following the revolution of 1848, whose failure—and subsequent hammer blows of political repression—made clear that this was no country for the young and liberal. They came to the United States by the thousands, first settling in cities and towns along the East Coast. With no roots and much ambition, they then looked westward. Already familiar with the language and customs of their adopted country, hundreds of them went no further west than Minnesota.

Included in the baggage they carried to America, though, were their native land's culture and education. As the local historian Gunther Plaut observed, this early wave of immigrants "read German books and German poets; they had intellectual interests and were touched by German rationalism."[2] They were, in effect, the offspring not of Karl Marx but instead of Moses Mendelssohn, the German-Jewish philosopher whose writings helped inspire the *Haskalah*, or Jewish Enlightenment, in eighteenth- and nineteenth-century Europe.

Few individuals better exemplified these liberal ideals than Judah Wechsler, St. Paul's formidable rabbi who played a vital role in creating the Painted Woods settlement in the 1880s. Born and educated in Bavaria, Wechsler brought his rigorous training and progressive values to his Minnesotan congregation. Though he was not a member of the era's growing Reform movement, his tendency was deeply reformist, especially in his conviction that Judaism had to accommodate itself to the modern age. As he declared in his application letter to the Mount Zion congregation in 1879, "My life has been devoted to the cause of reform and progress within the pale of Judaism."[3]

Propitiously, the Greenbergs arrived in St. Paul in 1907, the fiftieth anniversary of the founding of Mount Zion, the city's first Jewish congregation. By then, though, the Jewish community had, like successive geological strata, thickened dramatically. The earliest residents, not surprisingly, were largely of German heritage who, in search of business opportunities, had already lived in and left cities and towns elsewhere in the country. As a result, they were not only at home in English, but they also felt at home in the United States. Many of them, moreover, hailed from the merchant class; once they arrived in St. Paul, they had the financial means to launch their own businesses.

By the end of the century, though, the German-Jewish community in the Twin Cities was dwarfed by repeated waves of Polish, Russian, and Romanian Jew immigrants. By 1907, the combined Jewish populations of the two cities had combusted, with approximately 5,500 Jews living in St. Paul, largely on the city's west side, while roughly five thousand were in neighboring Minneapolis.[4] No less combustible were the differences between the German and East European communities. The same tensions that thrummed between German and East European Jews in New York unfolded in St. Paul. The German Jewish had quickly made a place for themselves in the city's commercial and cultural lives. Gradually, perhaps inevitably, they shed the religious and communal traditions they had brought to the United States; their political views were liberal as, increasingly, were their social values. They not only spoke English, but they also, as the saying went, "thought American."

Speaking English—not to mention thinking American—was already a challenge for their East European coreligionists, whose backgrounds and circumstances were dramatically different. Uprooted from a world of Yiddishkeit, still speaking its language and steeping in its traditions, this new generation of Jewish immigrants was, in the eyes of the German-Jewish community, a potential danger. It was not the rise of anti-Semitism they feared. (Remarkably, the local press uses the word for the first time toward the end of the century in the context of events overseas—the Dreyfus Affair in France—and not at home.) Instead, they feared that they would lose the social gains they had made over the previous fifty years.

This admixture of cultures, according to Plaut, created an evolving "social constellation whose significance cannot be overestimated."[5] While the outsiders did not, at first, make distinctions among the solar systems and planets in this constellation, that was not the case for insiders. St. Paul's Jewish community was divided not just between ethnic and linguistic lines—German Jews flocking to reformist congregations like Mount Zion and Russian and Romanian tending toward Orthodox congregations like B'nai Yaakov—but also along professional lines. By and large, German Jews were ensconced in the city's commercial and, increasingly, cultural life, while East European and Russian Jews, relegated to manual and menial jobs at first, remained on the margins.

This division was, in part, due to the relatively sudden and massive influx of Jewish immigrants from the Pale of Settlement to the pavement of St. Paul in the 1880s. While there might well have been unparalleled opportunities in Minnesota for these new arrivals, German Jews had to devote much energy and money to these destitute and dazed coreligionists to help them along the way. So much so that, in 1882, an increasingly frantic Rabbi Wechsler declared, "Humanity and a common duty to care for the unfortunate refugees prompted us to all that was possible for these people. We have spent the last cent we could collect in this emergency."[6]

Along with such acts of compassion and comprehension, however, there were countervailing reflexes of differentiation and discrimination. To distinguish themselves from their East European brethren, who only slowly were surrendering their traditional clothing and customs, German Jews doubled down on reforming religious practices and embracing secular cultural practices. In 1887, *The American Israelite*, a Reformist newspaper, reported that many stores owned by German Jews in St. Paul remained open during the High Holidays while an increasing number of German-Jewish households celebrated Christmas. As one local observed, "There is little doubt but in our times in nearly all households, whether Jew or Gentile, the season is celebrated, for the simple reason that in Rome, as the Romans we must do."[7]

Conversely, the more recent East European congregations, largely concentrated in the city's west side, at first held fast, if not faster, to the Jewish practices and rules they had carried with them from the shtetls and ghettos. Ironically, the motivations of both communities, though opposed to one another, were grounded in the common fear of anti-Semitism. While the East European immigrants, still carrying the fresh wounds of the anti-Semitic violence that had exploded across the Pale, sought to isolate themselves from American society, the German-Jewish immigrants, worried that their exotic coreligionists would spark anti-Semitic sentiment among their gentile neighbors, sought to insert themselves more fully in that same society.

The Greenberg family, it appears, straddled these two worlds. When they first arrived in St. Paul in 1907, they moved into the house of Sam Yaffee, the *shamash* who had often stayed with them at the Garske homestead. Soon after, Philip found a house for his family, located at 519 Capitol Boulevard, one of the principal thoroughfares in Frogtown. The unusual moniker, translated from the German Froschenberg, issues from the area's original residents—the croaking colonies of frogs living in the local swamps. By the late 1880s, the swamps (and frogs) had been displaced by railroad-related industries and housing for its growing number of mostly German, Austrian, Hungarian, and Scandinavian workers. Though it was torn down in 1973, and there are no extant photos, the Greenberg house was a step up from the farmhouse. Built from wood and brick, it probably resembled the surviving Victorian-style frame houses in the neighborhood. While it did not have the grand views outdoors, it did have modest plumbing indoors—an improvement that must have been welcomed by the family.

Another change was that the new home, unlike the Garske house, was no longer the center of communal and religious activity. Those tasks were instead under the auspices of Mount

Zion, the Reform synagogue a short walk away on Summit Avenue. Nettie Greenberg Epstein's letter to Devora Stocker, our sole source of the family history, is silent on the synagogue the Greenbergs attended and the practices they followed at home. It is possible that the dietary laws they had kept on their isolated homestead gradually gave way to the more liberal, even secular, approach at Mount Zion. Unlike neighborhoods on the west side, where Jewish immigrants from Eastern Europe mostly gravitated in the last decades of the nineteenth century, Frogtown boasted a greater ethnic diversity, teeming with Irish, Italians, Germans, Swedes, and Poles. As we will see, the synagogue's rabbi, Isaac Rypins, was ideally suited for such a neighborhood.

The nature of Philip's eventual job in St. Paul undoubtedly familiarized him with this local and lovely mosaic of people. In her account, Nettie notes that the second eldest, Samuel, had left Devils Lake for St. Paul in 1906 "to find employment." While staying with the Yaffees, he found a "job in a department store." We do not know which store and how long he remained, but city records indicate that by 1922, Sam and his father, whose employment history until then remains shrouded, had clearly saved enough money to buy the Star Wet Wash Laundry on nearby University Avenue. Sam was the establishment's manager in 1922 but seems to have found another job in 1922, when Philip took over and remained there until his death on August 27, 1931. In a 1971 interview in the *Chattanooga Times*, Jacob reported that his father had opened the city's first moving-picture house.[8] There is, however, no record of Philip Greenberg having done so. Even if he had not, the Jewish peddler from Kishinev, who became a successful homesteader in North Dakota, thus finished his days as a successful businessman in a

Mechanic Arts High School, St. Paul, Minnesota

busy commercial district in St. Paul, his storefront sharing the same street with a speakeasy, a film studio, and a cigar factory.[9]

While much of the formal education of the older siblings took place in the one-room schoolhouse on the Dakotan plains—the school whose administrator, according to Nettie, was her father—the youngest Greenbergs were shaped by the public schools in St. Paul. It is significant that Jacob—along with his older sister Nettie—attended the Mechanic Arts High School (MAHS). Founded a decade before the Greenbergs moved to St. Paul, MAHS was the house that George Weitbrecht built. A graduate of Antioch College who had also attended Harvard, Weitbrecht was a trained chemist and devout Unitarian. As the school's first principal, he brought to his task an unwavering conviction that public school should be the crucible to forge immigrants into an enlightened citizenry equally familiar with vocational and liberal arts.

The education was rigorous. While the boys were required to take classes in shop, modeling, and mechanical drawing, and the girls—in a concession to the age's cultural and sexual prejudices—took instruction in home arts, all the students were also required to take eight semesters of English, a foreign language, mathematics, and four semesters of history and sciences. It is unclear whether Weitbrecht closely followed cultural and educational movements at home or abroad, but there is a remarkable resonance between the practical ideals of his curriculum and the ethos of the nearly contemporaneous Bauhaus movement in Germany. Not unlike the Bauhaus, the goal of the school's mechanical arts program was "to produce useful objects." Among the objects woodworking students were expected to build was a Morris chair, an exemplification of the unadorned aesthetic espoused by Bauhaus teachers. Weitbrecht's encouragement of the "free use of the imagination," leading them to embrace "simple harmony rather the Victorian clutter for home interior decoration," also aligns with Bauhausian principles.[10]

When Jacob began at the school in 1917, not only had it moved from its original location—the basement of another high school in downtown St. Paul—to a new building on East Central Avenue, but it had also changed its name to George Weitbrecht Mechanic Arts High School. The school's name change was at the behest of Rabbi Rypins of Mount Zion synagogue. In 1916, following the sudden death of Weitbrecht, Rypins gave the closing sermon at his funeral. Having praised his friend's attachment to sincerity and allergy to "anything that was false and who worshiped the truth wherever he found it," Rypins proposed naming the school after Weitbrecht. A year later, when Jacob stepped through the school's front door, the paint for the new name was as fresh as the sorrow and sense of loss among the older students and staff.[11]

For the several hundred mourners at Weitbrecht's funeral, the sight of Rypins offering the closing sermon was hardly unusual or unexpected. Not only did the religious and ethnic diversity of the school's population mirror that of the neighborhood, but Rypins, who had long championed interfaith services and exchanges, was a pillar of the city's cultural and social worlds. Though born in Poland, he was trained at Hebrew Union College in Cincinnati, which encouraged his liberal and ecumenical bent. When he arrived at Mount Zion in 1889, Rypins proved as energetic, progressive, and, at times, controversial as his predecessor, Judah Wechsler. Convinced that a new generation of American Jews no more needed a knowledge of Hebrew than a knowledge of Aramaic to flourish in their new home, he removed it from the religious school curriculum.

Less successful, however, was his effort to align Mount Zion with the many Lutheran and Catholic churches in St. Paul by shifting observance of the Sabbath from Saturday to Sunday. After a few experiments in this direction, an increasingly recalcitrant congregation finally persuaded Rypins that this was a progressive bridge too far.[12] But these setbacks did not diminish his authority or popularity among his congregants and non-Jewish constituency. When Mount Zion reappointed Rypins to a new five-year term in 1916, an editorial in the *St. Paul Daily* hailed the news, noting that the rabbi had become "one of the most forceful and public-spirited of our citizens." What made him a notable "representative of his race and religion," the editorial concluded, is that Rypins is "none the less a Jew because he is truly American."[13]

Not surprisingly, the city's Orthodox Jewish community was less taken by Rypins's personality and politics than were their non-Jewish neighbors. We can only wonder if Jacob's parents shared the diffidence of their fellow Orthodox Jews toward Rypins. Paradoxically, while Philip and Mollie cleaved to Jewish law and customs on their homestead, their relative isolation from outside influences eased such a commitment. Once the family had settled in Frogtown, though, they and, more importantly, their children had to negotiate a world so unlike the one they had left behind in the Badlands. Their neighborhood was populated by a rich variety of cultural and religious communities—the many ingredients that, helter-skelter, had been joined in the national melting pot.

There were few purer distillations of this social and ethnic stew than the George Weitbrecht Mechanical Arts High School. Not only was the school's curriculum practical and progressive, but its student body was coed and racially integrated. (In fact, it was the only high school in St. Paul equipped with an elevator to accommodate disabled students.) "In the pupils of Mechanic Arts," one student proudly declared in the 1919 school yearbook, "you find democracy exemplified. Here is a working model of the melting pot. Rich and poor, Jew and gentile, bourgeoisie, proletarian and aristocrat, are on one plane of equality."[14]

The student neglected to include "Black American." Two years before Jacob enrolled at the school, Roy Wilkins had begun his studies there. A native of St. Paul, Wilkins attributed his future role as director of the NAACP from 1955 to 1977—a momentous era during which, in close association with Martin Luther King Jr., he helped to plan the Selma to Montgomery marches and played a pivotal role in the Civil Rights Act of 1964 and Voting Rights Act of 1965—to the education he received at MAHS. From his pre-engineering classes, Wilkins went on to become the editor of *The Cogwheel*, the aptly named literary magazine, and was named the salutatorian of the graduating class. Close to where the school once stood—which he described in his autobiography *Standing Fast* as the "best school in the city"—now stands a memorial to Wilkins titled *Spiral to Justice*.[15] Apropos of justice, yet another student at the school was Harry Blackmun, who began his studies there the year after Jacob's graduation. As Linda Greenhouse revealed in her 2005 biography, *Becoming Justice Blackmun*, had it not been for the unsolicited recommendation from two of his English teachers at MAHS, Blackmun would not have won the scholarship he needed to attend Harvard. And had it not been for Harvard, it is doubtful Blackmun would have eventually made his way to the Supreme Court, where he authored the epochal *Roe v. Wade* decision.[16]

A century later, with no family members to interview or family memoirs to study, we can only speculate on how the four years he spent at this remarkable school might have influenced the young Jacob Greenberg. At the very least, there is an unusual continuity between the homestead and high school experiences. The practical skills that Jacob acquired at MAHS were, in effect, the institutionalization of the skills that his father and older brothers had acquired on their own on the homestead. But whereas nature and necessity were his father's teachers, Jacob's teachers were men and women who, along with their specific areas of knowledge, also brought intellectual openness and inclusiveness to their classrooms. It may well be, for example, that one of Jacob's teachers had been Mary Copley, an attentive and compassionate English instructor cited by Wilkins as one of the pivotal influences in his own life. More broadly, the glories and miseries of the school's demanding curriculum and its extracurricular activities—Jacob probably played the viola in the MAHS orchestra—necessarily drew the young Greenberg away from the insular confines of his family and toward a spectrum of opportunities as dazzling and broad as the horizon of the Dakota plains. Indeed, his character and ambitions were undoubtedly shaped as much, if not more, by "the best school" in St. Paul than his family's experiences in the Badlands.

By the time Jacob graduated from MAHS, however, a growing number of fellow Minnesotans had recoiled at the very idea of the melting pot. Rather than a measure of the country's excellence, the great waves of immigrants to these shores were instead the measure of our decadence. This nativist reflex was ignited not by Protestant immigrants from Western and Central Europe but instead by Catholic and especially Jewish immigrants from Eastern Europe and Russia. As the historian John Higham observes in his landmark study of immigrants to America, *Strangers in the Land*, "The Jews faced a sustained agitation that singled them out from other new immigrant groups blanketed by racial nativism—an agitation that reckoned them the most dangerous force undermining the nation."[17]

This agitation was unusually strong in Minnesota—a development that must have been especially surprising to families like the Greenbergs, who had first passed through North Dakota. On the northern plains, anti-Jewish sentiment was as rare as winters that were clement. Rachel Calof makes no mention of anti-Semitism in her memoirs; blizzards, not pogroms, kept her awake at night. Similarly, the only racist incident that Sophie Rupin recounts from her childhood is when another child shouted "Christ killer" at her. "I said nothing," she recalls. "What was there to say? This was no Czarist Russia; we were not hiding in the attic. We were in America and this was just a stupid little girl."[18]

But such stupidity nevertheless took root in Minnesota during the interwar years. The state economy, based on agriculture and timber, did not enjoy the brief financial and industrial boom in other parts of the country. The burgeoning nativist and protectionist movements, deprived of the external enemies with the end of World War I, turned inward in their pursuit of those responsible for festering economic distress. The two World Wars bookended a period of mounting anti-Semitism throughout the country. Yet, the rise of anti-Semitism failed to spur a unified and urgent response from American Jewry. The reasons, according to Leonard Dinnerstein, were several. While German and East European Jews tended to point the finger at one another for growing anti-Jewish sentiment, local and national Jewish organizations, determined to keep a low profile, were reluctant to publicize their concerns. Better to maintain cordial relationships with their gentile neighbors than suggest some Christians cite their faith to justify their anti-Semitic beliefs.[19]

Xenophobic fears, fanned by populists and demagogues, spurred the passage of the Immigration Act of 1924. Lowering the percentage of immigrants allowed into the country from 3 to 2 percent, the act placed especially severe constraints on those seeking to emigrate from Eastern Europe. For both

German and East European Jews already in Minnesota, the consequences were also significant. In the years immediately after World War I, Jews were almost entirely excluded from social and civic organizations in some, but not all, parts of the state. For example, while such exclusionary policies were widespread in Minneapolis, they were much less so in its twin city, St. Paul. In 1922, Maurice Lefkovits, a prominent Minneapolis rabbi, shattered the omertà over these practices, declaring that "Minneapolis Jewry enjoys the painful distinction of being the lowest esteemed community in the land so far as the non-Jewish population of the city is concerned."[20]

These exclusionary practices were not restricted to social organizations. Burdened by sensationalist accounts of the activities of Jewish mobsters in local papers, Jews seeking jobs and housing in the Twin Cities increasingly ran into obstacles. This was the case for both skilled and unskilled Jewish residents. As for those with university degrees, there was no guarantee of landing white-collar jobs; instead, they often met with evasive responses or courteous rejections. A local historian, Laura Weber, notes that even professional Jews who launched their own businesses to pierce this wall of polite animosity could not always find offices to rent. In Minneapolis, several buildings applied a quota system to limit the number of offices rented to Jews, while yet other buildings refused to rent to them at all.[21] Though there were liberal ramparts in Minneapolis, the powerful and predominant Protestant community—the principal source of its anti-Semitic practices—commanded the city's social, economic, and political heights. This dreary situation led local Jewish leaders to create what one historian has described as "parallel" social and economic organizations.[22]

In fact, the systematic social and professional anti-Jewish discrimination found in Minneapolis eventually attracted the attention of the national press. In 1946, the muckraking journalist and lawyer Carey McWilliams shook the local elite when he published an article on their city in *Common Ground* magazine. Marveling at the contrast between the lot of Jewish Americans in St. Paul and Minneapolis, McWilliams declared, "One might even say, with a measure of justification, that Minneapolis is the capital of anti-Semitism in the United States." In every walk of life, he continued, "an 'iron curtain' separates Jews and non-Jews. Nor is this 'iron curtain' a matter of recent origin; on the contrary, it seems to have always existed. So far as I know, Minneapolis is the only city in America in which Jews are, as a matter of practice and custom, ineligible for membership in the service clubs." Even the local chapter of the Automobile Club, McWilliams exclaimed, refused Jews as members.[23]

As McWilliams and other observers noted, Minneapolis was, at first, an anomaly, a disturbing exception to an otherwise reassuring political, social, and economic landscape. While there were instances of implicit anti-Semitism in the local press, Henry Ford's explicit racism, blared by his newspaper, the *Dearborn Independent*, seems to have found few readers in St. Paul.[24] Similarly, while there were reports of Jews refused housing and jobs in St. Paul, they were few and sporadic. As a result, there was scarcely a diaphanous drape, much less an iron curtain that seemed to divide St. Paul. Several factors created this relatively enlightened status quo. First, Jews of German origin were more plentiful in St. Paul than in Minneapolis. Their material circumstances and secular background had translated into smoother social and economic integration, one that helped to buffer the subsequent shock of Jewish immigrants from Eastern Europe and Russia.

Second, the impact on public sensibilities of figures like Isaac Rypins, though impossible to measure, must have also played a critical role in St. Paul's greater openness to immigrants marked by such different appearances and attitudes. No member of the Jewish community in Minneapolis seems to have been equally impassioned and impressive as Mount Zion's rabbi. Third, St. Paul's ethnic and religious diversity, reflected in the student body and faculty ethos of MAHS, diluted the influence of the local Protestant community. Tellingly, there was also a higher percentage of Catholics in St. Paul than in Minneapolis. This proved decisive with the post-World War I resurgence in the northern states of the Ku Klux Klan, partly spurred by the impact of D. W. Griffith's revisionist and racist epic *The Birth of a Nation*, first released in 1915. The subsequent growth of the KKK in Minnesota could not help but draw together St. Paul's Jewish and Catholic communities. But as Jacob must have discovered when he left MAHS and entered the University of Minnesota in the fall of 1923, the forces of anti-Semitism did not always manifest themselves in the daft yet dire garb of the KKK.

In 1862, when the University of Minnesota was founded as a land-grant institution, there was but a handful of Jewish pioneers settled in the state. By the end of the nineteenth century, however, a growing number of Jewish students, largely of German stock, were attending classes at the St. Paul and Minneapolis campuses. While their numbers slowly increased in the years prior to World

War I, they were soon joined by a widening stream of young men and women like Jacob Greenberg, whose parents had fled the Pale of Settlement in the 1880s. By the end of the 1920s, when about twenty-five thousand Jews now lived in the Twin Cities, five hundred or so of their offspring were enrolled in the university's undergraduate and graduate programs.

For more than a few of these students, however, acceptance *by* the university was not tantamount to acceptance *at* the university. Unable to breach the high walls of the fraternity and sorority system, Jewish students at the university, following the model established in Minneapolis, founded parallel fraternal and preprofessional organizations, including chapters of the Menorah Society, first established at Harvard in 1906; a women's literary society, Scroll and Key, based on Yale's well-known secret society; and a chapter of Hillel in 1923. Though there were no explicit quotas, a member of the medical school faculty noted that the administration's attitude toward Jewish students shifted after World War I, with fewer applicants now being accepted.[25]

Moreover, the boarding houses that let rooms to university students often refused to accept Jewish women. The case of Miriam and Jeanette Calmerson, sisters who entered the university the same year as Jacob, is illustrative. Upon applying for a room at a boarding house near the campus, the owner turned them down because they were "of Jewish descent." When a friend of the Calmersons pressed the owner to explain her statement, she replied that "too many Jews" in a boarding house would lead the university's housing office to drop its ranking. Shockingly, if not surprisingly, this practice, aimed at Black as well as Jewish students, lasted well into the 1950s.[26]

Perhaps the most startling instance of this anti-Semitic strain that persisted at the university was the Luther affair. In 1935, Nazi Germany's ambassador to the United States, Hans Luther, undertook a tour of Midwestern cities and universities. Rotund and bald, Luther resembled a Georg Grosz portrait of a bloated banker (which happened to have been one of his earlier jobs). Indeed, Luther embodied the ideals of German bureaucracy: thoroughness and meticulousness. He also exemplified what Hannah Arendt, in her account of Adolf Eichmann, named "thoughtlessness"—the inability to "think from the standpoint of somebody else."[27] He was, as Arendt would argue, the most mediocre—indeed, banal—of men, committed to following official orders and not moral convictions. Not surprisingly, a puzzled biographer, having searched for Luther's ethical core, came up empty-handed, concluding, "Perhaps there was no core."[28]

Luther had served in a variety of prominent roles during the short life of the Weimar Republic, including stints as chancellor and president of the Reichsbank. Upon being named chancellor in 1933, Hitler appointed him as ambassador to Washington. Who better than this bland and benign bureaucrat to serve as a front to his regime's racist policies? Luther's reassuring message to his selected audience, Americans of German descent, was that his government practiced neither religious discrimination nor political persecution. Even if it did, these were "internal matters" that concerned his government, not those of other countries.

As spontaneous and scripted acts of violence against German Jews mounted in 1933, Luther, infuriated by criticism from the State Department, continued to insist that events were being misrepresented or manufactured by a hostile press. More than a few Americans seemed to share his perspective: When he appeared at the annual German Day celebration held at Madison Square Garden in New York, the crowd greeted him with a boisterous "Heil Hitler." A beaming Luther returned the greeting with a Nazi salute. Other venues, however, were less welcoming. When Luther gave a speech at Columbia University later that same year, he was met by more than two thousand protesters, shouting, "Herr Luther, why were books by Columbia professors burned in Germany?"[29]

By 1935, Secretary of State Cordell Hull was thoroughly exasperated by Luther's persistent denials of this new reality. Informing the American ambassador to Germany, William Dodd, that Luther "seemed to be a complete convert to Hitlerism," Hull scaled back his department's efforts to pressure the anti-Semitic policies of the Nazi state.[30] At the same time, Luther launched his Midwestern tour, determined to sell German American audiences on the benefits of free trade policies with the Third Reich. He did so despite the passage of the Nuremberg laws, which stripped German Jews of citizenship and relegated them to subjects of the Nazi state, and the "Night of the Long Knives," the massacre of remaining opponents to the Nazi regime, which included figures once close to Luther.[31]

The tour turned out to be a checkered affair. At the University of Wisconsin, a massive crowd of protestors formed outside the building where Luther was to speak. The Nazi ambassador denied that his government was persecuting German Jews and refused to discuss the matter with students and faculty, declaring, "I do not intend to answer special questions."[32] A few days later, Luther received a very different reception at the University of Minnesota. Not only was he treated to tea at the German Department, but he was also allowed to speak at the campus's large auditorium, Shevlin Hall. When a group of about fifty students, determined to question Luther about the atrocities unfolding in his country, arrived at the hall, they were prevented from entering by one of the university deans. When one of the students refused to leave the hall, police were called to remove him forcibly.[33]

By 1935, not only had Jacob Greenberg received his bachelor's degree in business from the state university, but he had also left the state. Moreover, he left the scantiest of paper trails: No extant personal correspondence involving Jacob nor official records concerning Jacob exist. This phase of his life is, as a result, almost entirely swathed in obscurity. Perhaps an observation made by the historian Riv-Ellen Prell applied to him: "Much like their parents, Jewish students learned to live within a world of diminishing opportunity in 1920s and thirties Minnesota."[34]

Yet, how diminished did this world seem to Jacob? Though he remained at home during his four years at the university, he was also deeply involved in extracurricular activities. Aligning with his professional interests, Jacob was a member of the university's Commerce Club, Music Club, and a violist in the symphony orchestra and the jazz band. Despite an administration that was either indifferent or hostile to Jewish students, Jacob and his fellow Jewish students managed to live full lives. In fact, Jacob's name was figured on the front page of the October 9, 1924, edition of the student paper, the *Minnesota Daily,* as the conductor of the seven-piece swing band that would perform that day on campus.[35]

GORDON GRAFF . . . . Sioux Falls, S. Dak.
Academic
Phi Kappa Sigma.

RAY GRAFF . . . . Sioux Falls, S. Dak.
Academic
Phi Kappa Sigma.

MYRTLE GRANDE . . . . Virginia, Minn.
Education

LOUISE GRANGER . . . . . . Rochester, Minn.
Academic
Delta Gamma; Skin and Bones; 1925 Gopher Staff; Tam O'Shanter.

RUTH A. GRANGER . . . . Minneapolis
Education
W. S. G. A.; Y. W. C. A.

C. M. GRAFF . . . . Minneapolis
Dentistry

J. RUSSELL GRAVES . . . . Duluth, Minn.
Chemistry
Chi Delta Xi; Chemist's Club.

FRANKLIN D. GRAY . . . . . . Minneapolis
Academic
Theta Delta Chi; Class Pres. 1, 2; Frosh Commission, Sec.; Soph Commission, Vice Pres.; Division Commander Stadium Drive; Masquers 1, 2, 3, Treas. 2, Pres. 3; Academic Council; 1925 Gophe Business Staff.

MARIAN J. GRAY . . . . . . Fergus Falls, Minn.
Academic

ABRAHAM L. GREENBERG . . . . . . St. Paul
Dentistry
Beta Delta Phi; Menorah Society.

JACOB GREENBERG . . . . St. Paul
Business
Music Club; Commerce Club; Symphony Orchestra; Band Orchestra; Concert Band.

MAURICE GREENE . . . . St. Paul
Dentistry

Battle Creek—Ramsey County

Page 152

University of Minnesota 1926 Yearbook
Photo of Jacob Greenberg in lower left corner

It was also at the university that Jacob met Lurine Karon, the fellow student who would become his first wife. The daughter of Arnold Karon, a successful investment banker in St. Paul, Lurine flourished at the university. A member of the Key and Scroll Society and secretary of the Menorah Society, Lurine also belonged to the Music Club. It seems a safe wager that she not only met Jacob at the club but that he was in the audience when

Lurine, an accomplished pianist, headlined a Mozart, Schubert, and Chopin recital on campus in 1926.[36]

Upon leaving university and home, Lurine would continue her piano education at a conservatory in Leipzig. As for Jacob, he would continue his graduate education at Columbia University in New York. His photo in the university yearbook shows a young man with his head tilted slightly downward. A warm smile cuts across the skin's dusky complexion, his face radiating confidence and pride. It is not difficult to believe that these traits were the result not just of the hardscrabble years in North Dakota and the heady days at MAHS but also the knowledge and skills acquired at the University of Minnesota. How ordinary it seems, yet how extraordinary it truly was that the son of an East European Jew—an itinerant peddler in Kishinev who became a small business owner in St. Paul—was about to launch into a life of remarkable professional and cultural accomplishments.

CHAPTER 3

THE APPRENTICESHIP OF A COMMERCIAL PIONEER

The man who sells has come to realize that he has a very definite responsibility toward the man who buys.

—JULIUS ROSENWALD

Economic geography seeks to describe and explain the absolute and relative location of economic activities, and the flows of information, raw materials, goods, and people that connect otherwise separate local, regional, and national economies.

—DICTIONARY OF HUMAN GEOGRAPHY

In the fall of 1927, Jacob began graduate studies at Columbia University in New York City. This appears to be his first visit to the city his own father's family failed to make home upon their arrival in the United States a few decades earlier. Though it lasted just one year, the transition from a city of about two hundred thousand residents to one of more than five million must have left a lasting impression on the young man.

The impression was all the sharper as New York City's largest foreign-born group, numbering over half a million, was Russian Jews. Along with the older German Jewish community, this population played a vital role in shaping the character of the nation's largest city. This impact, the sociologist Nathan Glazer suggests, distinguished New York from other global cities like London or Paris. "The issue of course is not just that New York is ethnically unrepresentative, it is that a marked distinctiveness in political orientation, occupational pursuits, and cultural tastes distinguishes American Jews from their fellow Americans."[1]

When Jacob moved into Hartley Hall, a campus dormitory located between 115th and 116th Streets, he had already decided on his field of study.[2] A graduate student in the business school, he focused on economic geography, a subfield of economics also known as geographical economics. Like a river splintering into a delta, the field has fragmented into yet smaller subfields since the 1920s. When Jacob entered Columbia, this branch of economics emphasized the nuts and bolts—or, rather, the natural and human resources of a specific region—of geography over the formulas and theories of economics. It was a practical approach to how regions, through the flows of information, resources, and people, are connected to one another.

It was, in short, the sort of discipline that would attract a young man born on a homestead and schooled at the Mechanic Arts High School. Among the courses Jacob could take at Columbia were Economic Geography of North America, The Geographic Factor in Economic and Social Development, and

Problems in Economic Geography and Foreign Trade.[3] Each of these classes anticipated the course of Jacob's subsequent business career as well as his own peregrinations from the northern plains to the Midwest, from the East Coast to the Great Lakes, then to the South and deeper South.

The graduate course of study at Columbia's business school was intense and demanding; much had to be covered in a single academic year, leaving little time for extracurricular pursuits. Unlike the University of Minnesota, where he was an officer in the Commerce Club and Music Club, played in the university orchestra, and led a swing band, Jacob did not join similar organizations at Columbia. With Lurine, whom he would marry in 1929, taking private cello lessons in Leipzig, Germany, Jacob seems to have been a man in a hurry, keen on launching himself into the world of commerce.

There were other venues, however, where he might have pursued his love of jazz and swing. On the city's Upper West Side, the Columbia campus is a short walk across Morningside Park to Harlem. By the 1960s, the park had become a racial flash point, dividing an elite and overwhelmingly white university seeking to expand and an overwhelmingly Black neighborhood seeking to survive. Forty years before, though, the sights and sounds of the Harlem Renaissance rose over and rolled across the park. How could the leader of a swing orchestra in placid St. Paul not walk twenty blocks north to 133rd Street, better known as "Swing Street," and slip into one of the dozens of interracial jazz clubs shouldering one another along the busy sidewalks?

While we can only conjecture about Jacob's experiences at the nearby jazz clubs, we can establish with certainty another and very different kind of musical experience he had even closer to Hartley Hall. In 1906, the Hungarian Jewish Orthodox congregation Ohab Zedek, whose first home was in the Lower East Side, erected a new synagogue on 116th Street. Built in (a relatively restrained) Gothic Tudor style, the pile was home not just to one of the city's most prominent rabbis, the Hungarian-born Philip Klein, but also to the world's most prominent cantor, Yossele Rosenblatt. Later in life, Jacob would often marvel over Rosenblatt's "gorgeous voice."[4]

While Jacob must have attended performances at the synagogue along with hundreds of other Jewish and non-Jewish visitors, it is possible that he also saw Rosenblatt—standing motionless on center stage, his enormous black beard framing his bespectacled face—at other venues, including Carnegie Hall, singing religious songs of his own composition. Perhaps Jacob even saw Rosenblatt on-screen at a local movie house that was showing Hollywood's first talkie, *The Jazz Singer*, in 1927. Remarkably, Rosenblatt had turned down an offer of $100,000 to play Jolson's father in the film, insisting it would violate his calling as a cantor. In desperation, Warner Brothers relented and created a scene, one with little bearing on the plot, where Rosenblatt appears as himself.[5]

No less remarkable, while Rosenblatt was performing to enraptured audiences just north of Columbia, a student a cappella group was singing anti-Semitic ditties to a smiling audience of fraternity brothers on campus. The historian Mark Oppenheimer discovered one song in their repertoire, punctuated with the refrain "the sheenys will go to hell," that pretended to explain how Jews controlled the university. Not surprisingly, the opposite was the case. Perhaps more so than at Minnesota, anti-Semitic reflexes shaped the worldview of Columbia's administrators. The irony, Oppenheimer observes, is that Columbia and the other Ivy

League schools would not have become what they are without the spur of anti-Semitism. They were not born but became exclusive, selective, and expensive "as part of the effort to limit the percentage of Jews in the student body."[6]

Worried that they would lose the sons of patrician New Yorkers—known as the Knickerbockers—to their Ivy competitors, the Columbia administration even created a second campus in Brooklyn, Seth Low Junior College, in its effort to repress the number of Jewish students at the main campus. One alumnus of this short-lived experiment in separate and unequal education recalled that the Seth Low student population "was heavily Jewish, with a strong Italian minority. It was clear that the purpose of the school was to give bright youngsters of unacceptable social characteristics a Columbia education without too badly contaminating the elite young men of Columbia itself by their formal presence." This Jewish graduate was the famous and famously prolific science fiction writer Isaac Asimov.[7]

Later in life, Jacob never spoke about anti-Semitism at Columbia. It may be that he did not encounter any instances of such treatment. It may, instead, be the case of other Jewish students of the same generation—that he accepted anti-Semitism as the price of getting a degree, as Oppenheimer suggests was true for several Jewish alumni he interviewed. Or it was simply, as Joyce Greenberg remarks, that Jacob was too busy looking ahead to spend time looking back.

Indeed, when he completed his degree in economics at Columbia in 1926, Jacob was already looking ahead. Shortly after his graduation, he left for Chicago. The timing could not have been more propitious: Not only did Yossele Rosenblatt leave Congregation Ohab Zedek in that same year, but Julius

Julius Rosenwald, who oversaw the transformation of Sears, Roebuck from a catalogue to a department store

Rosenwald, a man who must have left a deep impression on Jacob, became president of the corporation that had hired Jacob after his graduation: Sears, Roebuck Inc.

Oddly, the mass retailer's 140-year history begins roughly at the same time as the mass migration of East European and Russian Jews to the United States. From its modest origins in the 1880s as a mail-order firm specializing in watches, the company, formed by Richard Sears and Alvin Roebuck, quickly morphed into a burgeoning business that sold a dizzying range of goods. Like the thousands of mostly Jewish peddlers, including Philip Greenberg, who hawked their wares to farmers, Sears, Roebuck responded to the needs and desires of its mostly rural customers. The fledgling company depended, however, not on horse and carriage but instead on new communication and transportation infrastructures like the telegraph and railroads, vividly illustrating the concepts taught in Jacob's courses on economic geography.

But Sears, Roebuck was a corporation unlike any other. Few commercial ventures in the United States better reflect the nation's character—partly because it helped to shape that very character—than did the mail-order company. The relationship between the company and client was dialectical: The former provided, quickly and cheaply, what the latter needed. Yet it also anticipated what the client, as their means and expectations grew, would want next. In this respect, Sears marked a dramatic departure from department stores like Marshall Fields and Macy's. As the historian and former Sears employee David Cohn remarked, the catalog "never leads, never crusades. It is based purely upon public acceptance of the goods it offers, and not until the public has clearly signified that it wants a thing does that thing appear in its pages."[8]

The problem, though, was that behind the heaven offered by the mail-order catalog was the hell created in the actual operation. The rapid success of the company, largely fueled by the advertising brilliance of Sears—a man far better at writing copy than balancing books—outstripped its ability to maintain its stocks. As demand surpassed supply, pandemonium reigned in the company's shipping and storage facility in Chicago. All too often, a client who ordered a suit in one size and color would receive a suit in another size or color. Compounding the chaos was the company's innovative return policy, allowing dissatisfied customers to send back purchases that scarcely resembled what they had ordered. By the mid-1890s, the distribution center often had larger piles of incoming returns than it did outgoing purchases.[9]

Given the helter-skelter organization at the firm's headquarters, little more could be expected. "With a business that was growing so fast," remarked a Sears employee in 1896, "that we were fairly dizzy, without any previously developed system for handling such quantities, you can imagine the confusion. Our shipping rooms were in a state of constant congestion and every warehouse in Chicago was choked with our goods."[10] That employee was Julius Rosenwald, a native of Springfield, Illinois—he was born one block away from Abraham Lincoln's house—who had bought a large share of the company in 1895. Like Sears and Roebuck—or, for that matter, his hero Lincoln—Rosenwald did not have a university degree. He did not even have a high school degree, dropping out after his second year to work with his uncles in the clothing business.

Though Rosenwald would always feel burdened by his lack of schooling, it did not prove an obstacle to his success in business. On the contrary. Good at numbers and good with people, he left New York for Chicago, where, in 1893, he founded a clothing business, Rosenwald & Weil, with two partners. Two years later, the company was approached by Richard Sears, who desperately needed someone to supply ten thousand suits for orders he had already received for stock that did not yet exist. Rosenwald assured him he could meet the request and, through New York connections, found a local manufacturer, Mo Newburg, who could meet the pressing time constraints of the massive order. That Newburg was able to do so because he ran a sweatshop is a grim detail Rosenwald's most recent biographer, Peter Ascoli, largely elides, while Gordon Weil addresses it directly in his history of Sears, Roebuck.[11]

It may be that the ghastly conditions that served as the basis for Rosenwald's business success led him to become one of America's great philanthropists. When Rosenwald left his own company in 1897 to bring order and organization to Sears, Roebuck, and Co., however, his immediate concern was less who made his goods than who bought them—namely, the customer. He started out overhauling the department he knew best, men's clothing, but soon brought his knack for clarity and coherence to the entire operation. Yet, only so much could be achieved in the company's existing facilities—a jumble of warehouses and offices that Sears leased when they needed to expand. In 1904, Rosenwald persuaded a reluctant Sears to construct a new plant on a forty-acre site that lay five miles outside the city center. Two years later, when the four buildings were finally completed, the contractor boasted that it was "the largest mercantile plant in the world."[12]

The new buildings brought not only sound organization to Sears—according to corporation myth, Henry Ford conceived his idea of the assembly line during a visit to the Sears headquarters—but also brought a new conception of the relationship between corporations and customers. Richard Sears was driven to sell as much as he could and given to exaggerating as much as he could—two traits that, upon combination, often proved explosive. The year after Rosenwald assumed control of the men's department, Sears conceived a sales campaign for a new sewing machine. Predictably, customers fell for the lure of "Send No Money"; no less predictably, Sears had failed to guarantee an adequate supply of machines. Yet, it was only when Rosenwald intervened, reminding his partner that he should not make promises he could not keep, that the campaign lurched to a stop. With admirable restraint, one of Sears's assistants remarked that the "ideologies, business tactics, and personalities of Rosenwald and Sears were poles apart."[13]

When Sears resigned as president in 1908, Rosenwald was immediately and unanimously elected to replace him. Rosenwald's ascendancy reflected the sentiments not just of the executives but also of the company's rank and file. While Sears was captivated by schemes to sell whatever came to his attention, Rosenwald was committed to schemes to show that the employees had his attention. A pioneer of "welfare capitalism," Rosenwald oversaw the building of a hospital at the Chicago site as well as a well-furnished library and well-stocked and inexpensive cafeteria for the company's eight thousand employees. He also imposed a new business ethos, one that ran counter to Sears's often dubious practices, by announcing that the first and most important rule at the store would be truth in advertising.

"Not long ago the general practice in business was to let the buyer look out for his own interests," Rosenwald declared in 1914. But this practice needed to change, he continued. "The man who sells has come to realize that he has a very definite responsibility toward the man who buys."[14]

For Rosenwald, this imperative was no less ethical than it was commercial, applying not only to what he always referred to as "the store" but to the world as well. By the time he became president of Sears, Rosenwald had thus begun to turn his attention from bringing money in to giving it away. "I really feel ashamed," he once confessed, "to have so much money." By the end of his life in 1931, he had gone a great distance in effacing that sense of shame, having donated $63 million to various charities and institutions.[15] At first, Rosenwald lent his support to Jewish causes, but he soon broadened his aim, making many pivotal donations to the University of Chicago, among many other places. Most importantly, after meeting the educator Booker T. Washington in 1911, Rosenwald played a pivotal role in Black American history. In the era of Jim Crow, he made colossal donations not only to institutions of higher learning, like the Tuskegee Institute, but also provided the funds for the creation of a program that led to the construction of more than five thousand Black secondary schools, still known as the "Rosenwald schools," across the American South.

It is not surprising that Jacob was attracted to Rosenwald's company. At Columbia, his classes in economic geography confirmed the professional ambitions he had harbored in Minnesota. Jacob was less taken by theory than by practicality, less interested in visiting the stacks of a library than the stocks of a warehouse. Though he might have been aware of the connection, Jacob's future looked back to his father's past in Traverse City and Kishinev: the selling of goods, especially textiles. Not as an itinerant peddler, however, but as a sales executive.

For Jacob, the choice between the two corporate titans in the clothing industry, Montgomery Ward and Sears, Roebuck, was not difficult to make. He must have admired the latter's combination of sound business and ethical practices and its emphasis on practical rather than fashionable clothing. (To the distress of Joyce Greenberg, Jacob's own taste in clothing was stubbornly plain, if not downright pedestrian.) More important, he deeply admired Rosenwald's character and accomplishments, a man who became president of Sears, Roebuck not despite but *because* he was Jewish. Rosenwald's business sense stemmed from a moral sense grounded in Jewish tradition and law. Soon after moving to Chicago, Rosenwald began attending Temple Sinai, a growing congregation led by the charismatic rabbi Emil Hirsch. He continued to do so for more than three decades, and his life and work were deeply marked by this connection. "Never once in all that time," Rosenwald recalled, "have I left the Temple without feeling that I had carried away some helpful or inspiring lesson which would not have come to me except for having placed myself under such an influence."[16]

Rosenwald was not alone. Just as thousands of Jews and non-Jews alike flocked to Yossele Rosenblatt's performances at the Orthodox synagogue Ohab Zedek, thousands of gentiles and Jews gathered at the Reform Temple Sinai to hear Hirsch exhort them to extend themselves to others. The most influential figure in Reform Judaism, Hirsch affirmed that the spirit of Judaism, distilled by its ancient prophets, was not in the "minutiae" of Jewish law but in the movement for social justice.[17] Appearing at a public meeting with the Black American academic and activist W. E. B. DuBois in 1911, Hirsch declared that "the American who harbors race prejudice is committing a crime against his Americanism."[18] Practicing what he preached, Hirsch worked closely with the Chicago social reformer Jane Addams to improve the lot of immigrant communities and challenged members of his own congregation who owned garment factories to improve the mostly grim situation of their workers. A passionate advocate for the social justice movement, Hirsch helped to shape Rosenwald's commercial and ethical convictions. His insistence that the seller had an ethical obligation to the buyer stemmed from Hirsch's insistence that all human beings not only have self-evident rights but that we also have self-evident obligations to one another.

By the time Jacob graduated from Columbia, he was also graduating, in a sense, from his modest Jewish Orthodox origins. Where better to make this transition than under the guidance of the man who, as one historian subsequently noted, "saved" Sears, Roebuck?[19] Of course, Jacob was under no illusion he would meet Rosenwald, much less be interviewed for a job by the great man. (With his health faltering, Rosenwald would soon retire, replaced by the dynamic—and anti-Semitic—Robert E. Wood.) When he arrived at the Chicago headquarters in 1927, however, Jacob was surprised to find that his interview would be by Max Adler, one of the store's vice presidents who was also Rosenwald's brother-in-law. At the interview, Jacob had yet another surprise: Before joining Sears, Adler had been a concert violinist in Chicago. (He played on a Stradivarius—a detail that was perhaps the seed to Jacob's purchase of his own Stradivarius several decades later.) Upon learning that Jacob was also a violinist, Adler asked him why he did not pursue a career in music. "Because my fingers," Jacob replied, "didn't always do what my head told them to do."[20]

Not surprisingly, Adler knew what to do and hired the young man. (It was among his last decisions at Sears: Like his brother-in-law, Adler retired in 1928 to pursue a career in philanthropy.) Jacob began his training in the department where all newly hired Sears executives, following Rosenwald's example, started their apprenticeship—men's clothing. It is unclear if he trained at the flagship store, which was built inside the massive distribution center, or one of the two other Chicago stores that had opened by 1927—products of the fast and furious construction of stores across the country under Woods's leadership. Equally unclear is the nature of his training. Jacob arrived at a transitional moment in the company's history as it pivoted from its mail-order origins to a retail store future. Whereas fewer than one thousand employees worked in the retail division in 1925, nearly thirteen thousand had joined their ranks by the decade's end. Trying to keep up with this explosive growth, it was only in 1928—the year after Jacob was hired—that Sears first introduced a managerial training program. Yet, even that program, according to the corporate historians Boris Emmet and John Jeuck, "never eventuated in anything very effective."[21] Without access to the corporate archives, we are left to speculate on Jacob's possible promotions and potential changes of departments, work evaluations, and corporate activities during the six years he spent at Sears.[22]

Unfortunately, so much more from the Chicago period of Jacob's life is blurred. In 1929, he married his Minnesota classmate Lurine Karon, who then moved to Chicago and gave piano lessons at their home. It was also during this period that their children, Abby and Philip, were born, respectively, in 1934 and 1936. But we know little else. As Jacob would join synagogues in the various cities where he settled, it is possible that he and Lurine became members at Temple Sinai. Yet, once again, we cannot say with any certainty since the congregation, which has since changed addresses, does not have membership records reaching back that far.[23]

Jacob's trail grows even fainter in 1933, the year he left Sears and moved with his family to Mount Carmel, in southeastern Illinois, a town of seven thousand residents. The population has not changed over the subsequent century. He proceeded to spend the next six years there, working at a garment store, Marx Clothing. But neither Marx Clothing nor Jacob Greenberg has left a trace in the local archives. As a result, we can only guess at the position Jacob held, not to mention his reason for leaving Chicago and Sears for a town hardly bigger than Devils Lake, North Dakota, and for a store as tiny as Sears was titanic. Is it possible that his departure was related to the change in fortune at Sears in 1932, soon after the company suffered its first (and only) downturn in profit? It seems that Jacob was given a raise at some point after the crash in 1929, a reward for his sales record even after the Great Depression settled on the country.[24] But that raise must have preceded the dramatic downturn in profits in 1932. In response to this decline, the company imposed a 20 percent salary cut across the board. In the company's annual report of 1932, Robert Wood reassures stockholders that "every effort has been made to exercise all possible economies."[25] It may be that Jacob, a father of two children, was dissatisfied with the salary cut. Or it is possible that he was less than eager to continue to work for a company that was no longer under the guidance of Rosenwald, who had died a year earlier.

Happily, there is one archival fragment that can explain a subsequent and even more decisive move. In 1939, Marx Clothing began to supply wool trousers and jackets to the US Army, which had begun to beef up its manpower and material in response to the dire events unfolding in Europe.[26] This also marked Jacob's last year at the store. It may have been that as a student of the ebb and flow of goods, Jacob sensed the explosive potential of this new market. He and his family headed south, ushering in a new chapter to his life: Oklahoma!

CHAPTER 4

OKLAHOMA!

And when this territory is a state.
And jines the union jist like all the others
The farmer and the cowman and the merchant
Must all behave theirsel's and act like brothers.

—RICHARD RODGERS AND OSCAR HAMMERSTEIN

Genuine western denims for all-American cowboys. "Tuffies Out of the West" are the finest authentic western blue jeans.

—OKLAHOMA CLOTHING MANUFACTURERS

On March 31, 1943, the musical *Oklahoma!* opened on Broadway. The creation of the lyricist Oscar Hammerstein, yoked to a string of theatrical flops, and composer Richard Rodgers, burdened by the death of his long-time collaborator Lorenz Hart, there was little advance fanfare. When the curtain rose on the shoe-string production

Rehearsal of original cast of the musical "Oklahoma!"

at the St. James Theater, the auditorium was nearly as empty as the stage on which a single, old woman was seated while churning butter.

Within a matter of days, however, the musical became the hottest ticket in town. Spanning more than two thousand performances, *Oklahoma!* also spanned the globe. As a war correspondent covering the brutal war in Italy in 1943, John Hersey recalled one morning, as the troops were beginning to awaken, that one of them began to sing, "Oh, what a beautiful morning!" There was an ironic edge to the soldier's voice, Hersey admitted, yet he insists that the morning had, through the prism of the music and lyrics, become beautiful. "All of a sudden, there was an almost unbearable intensity in the way the men looked around at the view."[1]

Oklahoma! transformed the American musical. Until Rodgers and Hammerstein appeared on the scene, musicals mostly drew on the vaudeville tradition of the Ziegfeld Follies: song, dance, and patter. With *Oklahoma!* this tradition was overtaken by narrative-driven drama that wove a story through song, dance, and dialogue. The stakes of this drama could not have been greater. In part, as Hersey reminds us, the musical gave a welcome jolt to a nation and people at war. A story of cowboys, courage, and the taming of the New World, *Oklahoma!* seamlessly meshed with the story of soldiers, courage, and the taming of an Old World savaged by totalitarian forces.

But the musical beats with yet another crucial subtext. Against the historical backdrop of the territory of Oklahoma achieving statehood, the musical's songs and dances portray the assimilation of this far-flung land into the union of American states. But no less powerfully, the musical also promotes the assimilation of immigrants to America into that same union. Striding across the stage are the iconic figures of the farmer and cowboy, but there is yet another crucial, if less heralded, fixture to the American West: the merchant who supplies the cowboy and farmer's tools and clothing. Despite allusions to his Persian background, Ali Hakim, the musical's merchant, is transparently Jewish. The number of Persian peddlers in the American West, as the historian Andrea Most drily notes, was "negligible, to say the least."[2] Tellingly, the play's director, Rouben Mamoulian, considered casting Groucho Marx in the role of Hakim. Ultimately, and no less tellingly, Mamoulian finally gave the role to Joseph Buloff, a star of Yiddish theater. At the play's climax, the flirtatious and fast-talking Hakim discovers, at first against his will, that he must marry a local girl and thus become part of the community. The meaning of this decision, as transparent as Hakim's Jewishness, is underscored by a dance number in which all the men, including Hakim, are corralled by women. Through the magic of a Broadway musical, the Jew as Other has become the Jew as American.

By the time *Oklahoma!* had settled in for its long run in New York, Jacob Greenberg had been settled for four years in the small Oklahoma town of Chickasha. Later in life, he was fond of remarking that there were just three Jewish families in Chickasha when he moved there with Lurine and their young children, Philip and Abby. Jacob was exaggerating, though not by much: in 1937, fewer than sixty Jews lived in the town.

This had not always been the case. Forty miles southwest of Oklahoma City, Chickasha's population in 1939 hovered just above fourteen thousand.[3] Founded in 1892 as a shipping hub for the newly built Rock Island Railway that shuttled wheat and cattle to Chicago, the town was built on land belonging to the Chickasaw Nation. Or, rather, *had* belonged: When Oklahoma became the forty-sixth state in 1907, it effectively annexed most of the land that now comprises Grady County, which Chickasha serves as the seat of government.

The demographic and economical critical mass required for statehood was triggered in 1889. That year witnessed the first of several Oklahoma land runs: the mad dash by caravans of prospective landowners across more than two million acres of so-called unassigned lands. This phrase was the bland descriptor for the prime real estate the American government carved from the land they had emptied of the half-dozen or so Native

American Nations that had lived there. Like North Dakota's Homestead Act a decade earlier, the Oklahoma land runs, which continued until the end of the century, drew tens of thousands of Americans to launch new lives by claiming title to 160 acres of free land that had cost its original residents dearly.

It is possible that the recently arrived Jewish immigrants from Eastern Europe drew parallels between the creation of the reservation system by the American Republic and the invention of the Pale of Settlement by Czarist Russia. But it is beyond question that the friction and fractiousness that existed between German and Eastern European Jews elsewhere in the United States were reenacted between the two communities in Oklahoma. Yet, these tensions played out on a smaller stage. Prior to the start of the land rushes, about one hundred Jewish settlers lived in the territory that would become Oklahoma. There is no official tally of Jews who were among the "boomers" and "sooners," but on the eve of statehood in 1907, it is estimated that the Jewish community stood at approximately one thousand. By the end of the 1920s, the state's Jewish population had climbed to 7,500—a demographic peak from which the community has ever since been descending. (In 2003, the five thousand Jews who resided in Oklahoma constituted 0.1 percent of the state's total population, a stark contrast to the national average of 3 percent.[4])

Whether of German or East European origin, most Jewish newcomers settled in the state's two largest cities, Oklahoma City and Tulsa, while smaller numbers trickled into towns like Muskogee and Seminole, Enid and Guthrie. While a few were in the liberal professions, most of the Jewish settlers sought to earn their livelihoods as shopkeepers and merchants. Like the

Froug mercantile dynasty, which established a chain of garment stores in several towns across the state, many concentrated on dry goods and textiles. The economic success enjoyed by these early settlers, fueled after 1900 by the discovery and exploitation of the region's vast oil reserves, laid the foundation for early congregations in the towns of Ardmore and Muskogee and, subsequently, in Oklahoma City and Tulsa. As in St. Paul and Minneapolis, so too in these towns: while German-Jewish settlers gravitated toward the Reform movement, East European Jews instead tended toward the Orthodox synagogues.

This modest stream of Jewish settlers to Oklahoma reached as far as Chickasha. In 1902, the Russian Jewish immigrant Benjamin Lubman, after a short time in Kansas City, moved to Chickasha and opened a haberdashery. He was followed by a handful of other Jewish merchants, including Herman Kohn and Abraham Belk, but Charles Miller and Ben Levine established the town's most enduring presence, with the opening, in 1919, of Dixie Store. The store won fame for its annual promotional campaign, Dixie Days, when Miller would toss live turkeys from the store windows.[5] Even before the arrival of Miller and Levine, the town's Jewish community was large enough to form a congregation, B'nai Abraham, conducting its services in the local Masonic Temple. Though small, the Jewish community in Chickasha no doubt expected even brighter days—expectations that nevertheless soon came to naught. The membership, having crested at twenty-five, soon declined steeply enough to lead to the congregation's dissolution by 1940.

When the Greenberg family arrived in Chickasha in 1939, the Dixie Store was still open for business. This was not the case, though, for the town's Jewish congregation, which seems to have closed its doors shortly after the Greenbergs' arrival. Under the impact of the lingering Great Depression and the festering of the Ku Klux Klan, many of Chickasha's Jewish residents could not resist the pull of nearby Oklahoma City. Thanks to the petroleum boom that began to reverberate across the state in the 1930s, Tulsa must have also drawn many Jewish residents from the state's smaller towns.

Jacob must have known that the move to Chickasha, when rural Oklahoma was still reeling from the Great Depression and Dust Bowl, seemed at best willful, at worst wrong-headed. He was recreating the frontier experience his parents knew in North Dakota or, for that matter, the experience of other immigrant Jews to the American West in the late nineteenth century. Once again, though, the absence of personal papers leaves us in the dark. (In the previously mentioned profile published by the *Chattanooga Times*,[6] Greenberg spoke at length about his six years in Chicago but passed over in silence the twenty-seven years he spent first in Chickasha, then Oklahoma City.)

The one extant document from their time in Chickasha is the 1940 edition of the city directory. (Unfortunately, the Grady County Historical Museum's series of directories has a gap between 1940 and 1947, by which time the Greenberg family had moved to Oklahoma City.) The family is listed as living in a house at 915 Twelfth Street—"a nice neighborhood," according to the archivist—and Jacob is described as the manager of Oklahoma Clothing Manufacturers, located at 223 Chickasha Avenue. The absence of relevant company or public documents

One in a series of history booklets distributed with "Out of the West" clothing

leaves unclear whether he was the owner as well as the manager in 1940 or if he eventually became the company's owner.

But the promise held by this garment mill was undoubtedly the reason for the family's move to Chickasha. When Marx Clothing began to supply trousers and jackets to the United States Army in 1939, it did not require a master's degree in economic geography to grasp the significance of this new market. With the build-up of the American military in response to the build-up of global tensions, Jacob understood that playing a role in meeting the nation's material demands was both a patriotic duty and a financial opportunity. In the first instance, individuals whose occupations were deemed essential to the war effort were given a draft deferment. This appears to have been the case for Jacob.

In the second instance, the clothing industry enjoyed a win-win situation during the war years. While the military had an enormous need for clothing and textile goods, these needs did not exhaust the industry's resources. Though it faced government controls, the garment industry was less affected than many other sectors of the civilian market that were hampered by material or political restrictions during the war. They also had a ready and eager clientele on the home front. With the wartime economy steadily lifting their wages, American workers were eager to spend their checks. Where better than the nearest department or general store? Predictably, civilian consumption of clothing rose between 1942 and 1946, while the production of woolen goods for the civilian market consistently exceeded that for the military during these same years.[7]

With the war's end, consumerism and optimism joined forces, creating a society, in the words of the usually staid historians at the Library of Congress, "more affluent in the

for
all-american
cowboys
Genuine Western Denims

NOW, with Zippers, Tuffies Out Of The West are the finest authentic western blue jeans. They're made of tough, 8-oz. Sanforized LANE denim, copper riveted, double-stitched with heavy orange thread, and with inside swinging pockets.

$2.29 pr.
Anywhere In U.S.A.

IN SIZES 1-22
20" to 32" Waist

Guaranteed by Good Housekeeping

ADVERTISED IN LIFE

TUFFIES OUT OF THE WEST
COWBOY PANTS

OKLAHOMA CLOTHING MFRS., Inc.
OKLAHOMA CITY 1, OKLAHOMA

TUFFIES OUT OF THE WEST

the Real West

Booklet 2 --- Cowboy Clothes

MAYBE sometime you might want to work on a big ranch out west . . . well, what we're fixin' to do now is to tell you all about real cow-riggin', which is what the cowboy calls his workin' clothes. Too many dudes show up on a "spread" dressed in range clothes in an exaggerated manner . . . cowboys refer to a "tenderfoot*" dressed like that as—". . . a mail order catalog on foot."

The cowboy's clothing was not homespun like the pioneers . . . it was trading post or store-bought. In style, however, it was adopted from the Mexican cowboy, the Vaquero (pronounced Vah-kayro). Most all cow-riggin' is designed the way it is because it fits into the cowhand's way of livin'.

Let's turn the page now and start in with the cowboy's hat . . . or, his "hair case", or "lid" as it is sometimes referred to.

* When whiteface hereford cattle were first introduced into the southwest, they had to walk the cattle great distances from the railroad. These cattle were not accustomed to hard ground like the longhorns were, and it was not long before their feet became sore. This led to the expression "tenderfoot"—now applied to all newcomers to the west.

One in a series of history booklets distributed with "Out of the West" clothing postwar years than most Americans could have imagined in their wildest dreams before or during the war."[8] While neither its economy nor population grew as quickly as many other states, Oklahoma was hardly exempt from the tidal forces sweeping across American society. The postwar years in Oklahoma witnessed a steady decline of the state's agricultural base and the concomitant growth of its commercial and industrial sectors. Not only did the state fully retire its prewar debt, but its per capita income also climbed dramatically.

A paradoxical yet predictable consequence of the burgeoning urbanization and modernization of Oklahoma was the idealization of frontier life. In popular culture, the state's arid landscape, now pockmarked by oil rigs, was transformed into a dreamscape. Across this stage rode the cowboy, the quintessential embodiment of an authentic America that we had abandoned. This was the mythic America portrayed, of course, by Hammerstein and Rodgers in *Oklahoma!* and in the movies and ads mass-produced by Hollywood and Madison Avenue. It was the way that the American West, including Oklahoma, never was, but that hardly mattered. What instead mattered is that the ideals and, by extension, symbols of this golden age were eagerly embraced.

Of course, examples of such advertising campaigns are as plentiful as the military campaigns against the Native American nations who had once hunted on this same land. This image of authenticity stretches from Phillip Morris's iconic Marlboro Man—who would light up while Elmer Bernstein's theme music welled up—to Ralph Lauren's Chaps. In its 1979 television advertisement, images of young men in trucks—as well as images of, well, Ralph Lauren—unspool as the voice-over

OKLAHOMA CLOTHING MANUFACTURERS

Mr. Jacob Greenberg came to Wewoka about 1944 and began the manufacture of men's clothing under the name of Oklahoma Clothing Manufacturers.

He made a contract with S. N. North in March 1946 for a five year lease on a building on West Cedar Street. The Chamber of Commerce helped raise money for repairs and alteration of the building. He was a successful operator and before the five year lease had expired negotiations were made for a new building which resulted in the completion in 1951 of the present brick building housing the company which now employs an average of 200 persons. Cost of the building was amortized through the Wewoka Industries, Inc., whose capital of $100,000 was raised by a group of citizens in Wewoka after a hard and difficult campaign.

The company, manufacturers of the famous Tuffies jeans, was sold by Mr. Greenberg and is now a subsidairy of the Puritan Fashions of New York City. Plans for another expansion are well under way and will double the present building and operations.

Oklahoma Clothing garment plant in Wewoka, Oklahoma

declares this is a "cologne a man can put on as naturally as a worn leather jacket or a pair of jeans. Chaps. It's the West. The West you would like to feel inside yourself."[9]

Under Jacob's guidance, Oklahoma Clothing Manufacturers tapped into this rich advertising tradition. The company produced and sold two lines of clothing, "Tuffies out of the West" for aspiring cowboys and "Ruffies out of the West" for ambitious cowgirls. No less ambitious was the ad campaign, which lassoed page space in *Life* and *Look* magazines, as well as the imprimatur of *Good Housekeeping.* In flyers sent to prospective retailers, Oklahoma Clothing made an impressive case for carrying its brands: The stores would be protected from any losses as well as by the company's promise to sell their products only to better retailers. As the flyer explained, the products would be "sold exclusively to upstairs departments of better independent stores. No basement, chain store or cut-price competition." Moreover, there was both the panache of its national advertising campaign—"You've picked the right brand, pardner!"—and the promise of "authenticity."

When it comes to jeans, there could be no greater sign of their authenticity than, as Oklahoma Clothing trumpeted, the copper riveting "at every point of strain." Similarly, there could be no sweeter sign of irony than that this very same authenticity was based on the original denim jean created in 1873 by Levi Strauss, the German-Jewish immigrant who had founded a dry goods company in California. The irony was compounded in 1941 when, following hundreds of customer complaints that the back rivets scratched their furniture and even saddles, the Levi Strauss Company began to cover the rivets.[10]

Boosted by various promotions, ranging from free Tuffies lollipops and pencils to a series of booklets recounting the history of "the genuine old west," the fortunes of Oklahoma Clothing Company rose as high as an elephant's eye. In 1945, Jacob moved his family from Chickasha to Oklahoma City. A few years later, he opened a second garment plant in Wewoka. At first glance, the choice of Wewoka, a small town in the heart of the Seminole Nation more than a hundred miles east of Chickasha, is obscure. At second glance, though, it was a canny move. During the interwar oil boom, the town's population had exploded, reaching more than twenty thousand in the late 1920s. But as the nearby oil deposits emptied, so too did the town. By 1950, Wewoka was one-quarter the size, with fewer than seven thousand residents.[11]

As a result, the town welcomed the construction of a new building for Oklahoma Clothing. Jacob's ties to Wewoka stretched back to 1944 when he leased an older building in the town to install a second garment plant. By 1952, business proved so brisk that Jacob had a new building erected, one large enough for two hundred workers employed by Oklahoma Clothing. The building, whose cost was amortized by $100,000 of capital raised by a local group of businessmen, opened in April 1952. That fall, the company welcomed the townspeople to tour, in the words of the *Wewoka Daily Times,* its "attractive and commodious structure." An editorial in the paper also urged children to visit the facility. Underscoring the economic boon represented by the plant, the editorialist opined that it was essential to the education of Wewoka's youth. "Part of our children's education," it declared, "should be an appreciation of the commercial enterprises which support the community and help make good school and other essential facilities possible. Children with such an appreciation grow into useful men and women."[12]

Jacob Greenberg and employee at the Oklahoma Clothing garment plant in Wewoka, Oklahoma

Oddly, a few months earlier, the plant had been the scene of an incident that was as authentically American as the blue jean. Representatives of the International Ladies Garments Workers Union had circulated a flyer accusing the plant's forelady of bullying the plant's workers. There are no extant sources, police or municipal, on the incident; as for the flyer, Jacob reprinted it in a speech he gave to the employees. (The speech was, at his request, transcribed and notarized by a court reporter.) Along with the accusation leveled at the forelady, the ILGWU flyer also affirms that while such intimidation passes for the norm in Soviet Russia, it will not pass in a free America.

Jacob's speech resonated with his anger at the accusation. He was born not in a Russian *shtetl*, he told his employees, but on a North Dakotan homestead: "I can tell you about our experiences on the farm, but I am glad I can't tell you anything about Russia." In a scarcely veiled allusion to David Dubinsky, Jacob added that "the head of this Union can tell you all about Russia" since he was born there. Based on a recent trip with Lurine, Jacob proceeded to recount the inroads made by communism across Europe, especially in France and Italy. He lamented the "lies and distortions and slurs" he saw and heard during his travels in Europe, "propaganda that has built up such a hatred for the Americans" and that resembled "the circulars passed out in front of this factory." Reassuring the workers that they could attend union meetings or join the union without fear of losing their jobs, Jacob concluded by affirming that he would continue to make "everyone who works in this factory feel that his job is secure." At the end of the speech, recorded the court reporter, the employees applauded.

The incident, which remains unclear and undocumented, and Jacob's response occurred during the Red Scare and the ascendancy of Senator Joseph McCarthy. As a result, the alleged accusations aimed at Jacob were radioactive. Moreover, as a Jewish American, Jacob was acutely sensitive to such baseless accusations. This explains, in part, the reason for and the rhetoric of his speech. Understandably, Jacob treasured his historical roots in the Badlands and the family memories and myths surrounding this chapter in his life. One can imagine his pride when, looking across the factory floor, he declared, "I was the son of a pioneer American farmer who broke virgin land in North Dakota at a time when our farm was twenty-five miles from the nearest town, and you covered that twenty-five miles with a team of oxen."

Nevertheless, Jacob's suggestion that Dubinsky was tainted by communism was as baseless as were the accusations against him made by local union organizers. In a recent biography, the historian Robert Parmet reaffirms what Dubinsky's contemporaries already knew: The ILGWU leader harbored a lifelong and "deep-seated hatred of Communism." In fact, in the same year that Jacob spoke to his employees in Wewoka, Dubinsky spoke to his rank and file at the ILGWU convention in Chicago, reminding them that their union had "been fighting Communism and the Communists since 1918"—an era, he added, when this position "wasn't fashionable."[13]

There is a tragic element to this misunderstanding. Dubinsky was no less a defender of capitalism than Jacob. "Trade unionism," he insisted, "needs capitalism like a fish needs water." Yet, while Jacob embraced a paternalist model, Dubinsky was more skeptical. "If we are going to keep free enterprise it must be made responsible. It must function in the public interest. Nobody but a lunatic could believe in a system that produces violent business cycles, mass unemployment, and misery for millions of people."[14] As the labor intellectual Gus Tyler remarked, Dubinsky not only spoke Yiddish, but he *thought* in Yiddish.[15] In other words, Dubinsky's worldview was shaped by the messianic tradition rooted in the Jewish experience in Eastern Europe. As for Jacob, he not only spoke American English, but he also *thought* in American English. His worldview, so very different from Dubinsky's, was shaped by both the reality and mythology of Western America. It was a worldview that Jacob, as restless as he was confident, would soon carry from Oklahoma to Texas.

Moses Soyer, "Bare-backed model"

Tang Dynasty horse, 8th century China

Otto Dix, "Flowers"

Max Pechstein, "Portrait of Lötte"

Ernst Wilhelm Nay, "Chromatische Phantasie"

Max Pechstein, "Rising Nude"

Käthe Kollwitz, "Self-Portrait"

Emil Nolde, "Poppies"

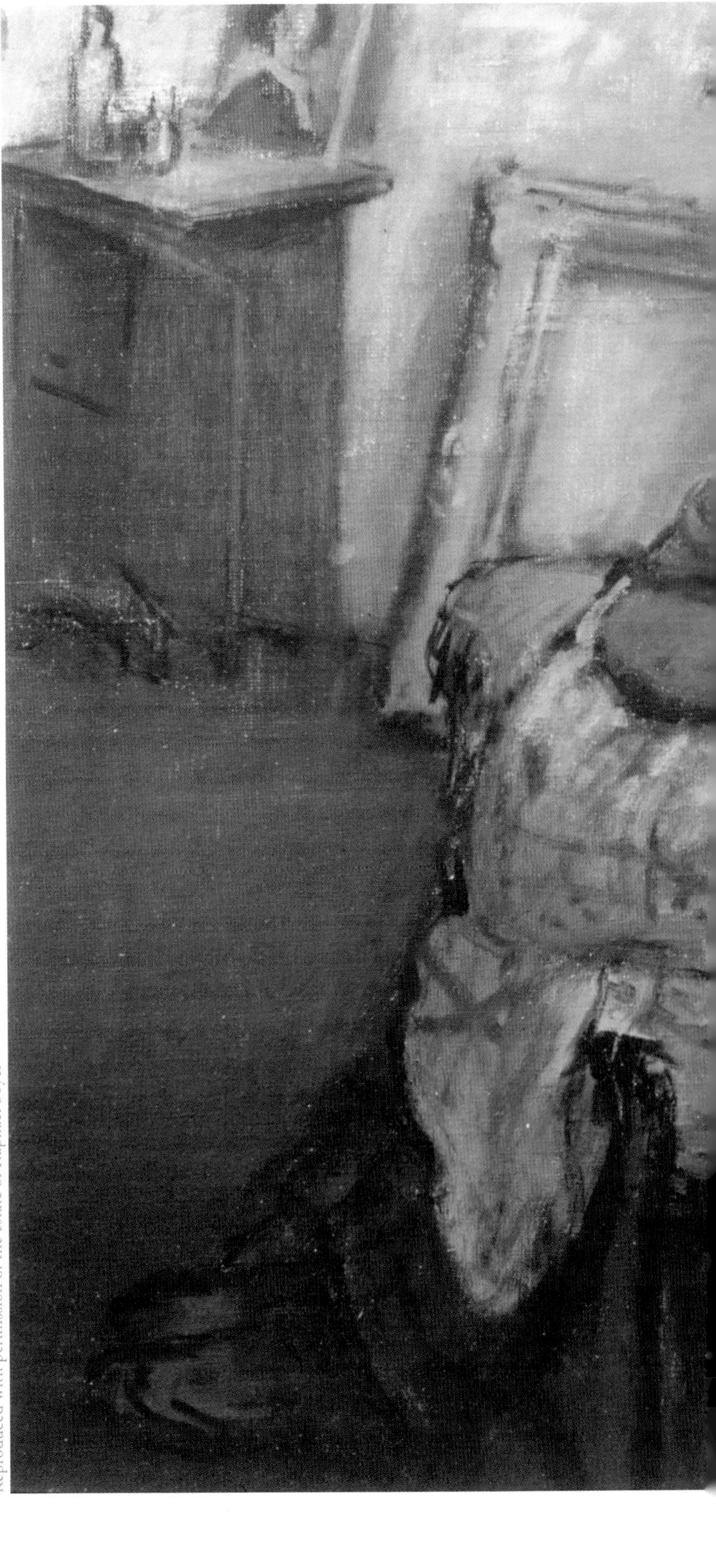

Raphael Soyer, "Couple sitting in an armchair"

Georges Raoult, "Acrobat and King" (two-sided painting mounted on a hinge)

Georges Raoult, "Figure Study" (reverse side of "Acrobat and King")

Ernst Wilhelm Nay, "Untitled"

Nay 55

Raphael Soyer, "Study for Homage to Eakins"

Moses Soyer, "Three Dancers"

Christian Rohlfs, "Gelbe Blüten"

CHAPTER 5

THE HOUSTON YEARS

All in all, Jacob was not a complicated man.
What you saw was what you got.

—RABBI DONALD ROSSOFF

By 1962, Jacob had clearly grown dissatisfied with the sewing and selling of clothing. This had been his world for more than three decades, stretching from his start as an employee in Chicago and Mount Carmel to his passage as an employer in Chickasha and Oklahoma City. But this history extends, in an important sense, even further back. Dealing in garments, after all, had also been his father's world, from Kishinev and Traverse City, where Philip had been a peddler, to St. Paul, where he became the owner of a laundry. It was time for Philip's youngest son, now approaching sixty, to break with this tradition.

This explains, in part, his decision that same year to sell Oklahoma Clothing Company to the expanding Puritan Fashions Corporation based in New York City. Just as Julius

Rosenwald and Max Adler did when they had realized their ambitions in the world of commerce, Jacob had begun, both figuratively and literally, to expand his horizons. Spending half the year abroad, Jacob and Lurine eventually traveled to some eighty-five different countries during their marriage. (It was their recent trip to St. Petersburg that led to the baseless suggestion, in the ILGWU pamphlet, that Jacob was a communist sympathizer.) By then, the number of charities to which Jacob donated rivaled the number of countries he had visited. Many of them were Jewish causes and institutions, yet others developed from his globe-trotting. At times, the two combined, as was the case with his generous support for the Jewish Heritage Council of the World Monuments Fund.

Jacob also managed to join his business and cultural interests. Whereas he had tapped into a partly historical and partly mythical past with his clothing line of Tuffies and Ruffies, he now turned toward modern cultural trends. His commissioning of a bowling alley in the mid-1950s was the most striking instance of Jacob's engagement with new movements in design. In 1958, he opened the 300 Bowl in downtown Phoenix—a stunning example of Googie-style architecture. This movement saw the light of day in the neon-lit nights of California diners in the early 1950s. Its trademark was a vaulting roof that topped a vast glass facade, a brilliant boomerang of reinforced concrete rising toward the sky, and, of course, riveting the attention of passing motorists. If that was not enough to catch the eye, there was inevitably a great and garish neon sign, inspired by Las Vegas casinos, flashing alongside the façade. The building still stands as the renamed Christown Lanes, praised as one of the few surviving examples of Googie architecture in Arizona.[1]

Photo of the "Googie" style 300 Bowl in Phoenix, Arizona

But this was not the first time Jacob had connected his financial and cultural interests. Six years earlier, he had made an investment not in the sun-drenched stretches of downtown Phoenix but in the still rubble-strewn streets of a divided Vienna. On April 26, 1952, T. E. Burch, the president of Security State Bank in Wewoka, received an airmail letter from one of his bank's most valued customers, Jacob Greenberg. In the letter, Jacob asked Burch to transfer $15,000 to a bank in Zurich, Switzerland. The equivalent of $170,000 today, this request was a significant transaction. While Burch's bank did not have the means to make an overseas transfer, he immediately replied to Jacob, assuring him that he would make the transfer through Chase National Bank in New York. Of course, Burch did not ask the reason for this transfer of funds. If Jacob had told him the reason, however, the Wewoka banker would undoubtedly have been surprised.

Jacob had posted the letter while he and Lurine were touring Europe—the same trip that included the visit to Russia that the IGLWU pamphlet subsequently misrepresented. Rather surprisingly, Vienna was among the cities visited by the Greenbergs. In 1952, Vienna was no longer the tourist destination it had been before the Anschluss of 1938 when Nazi Germany annexed Austria. Instead, it was a city still bearing the open wounds of the war. Streets had been reduced to piles of rubble, residents reduced to rationing, and the city itself reduced into four separate zones. Each was administered by the military and political representatives of the four countries allied during the war—the United States, Soviet Russia, Great Britain, and France—who also jointly administered the so-called international zone in the city's center.

When Jacob and Lurine arrived in Vienna, it still resembled the gray and grim cityscape featured in one of the century's most iconic and influential films, *The Third Man*. Directed by Carol Reed, written by Graham Greene, and starring (in a cameo role) Orson Welles, much of the film was shot in Vienna in 1948, just four years before the Greenbergs arrived. In the subsequent novella based on his screenplay, Greene's narrator describes Vienna as a "city of undignified ruins. . . . The Danube was a gray flat muddy river a long way off across the Russian zone, where the Prater lay smashed and desolate and full of weeds, only the Great Wheel revolving slowly over the foundations of the merry-go-rounds like abandoned millstones, the rusting iron of smashed tanks which nobody had cleared away, the frost-nipped weeds where the snow was thin."[2] The city was not just physical place but also a metaphysical place, a metaphor, as the historian Brigitte Timmermann argues, for "a world that had physically and morally fallen apart."[3]

The "Burmester" Stradivarius violin

It was Jacob's relentless curiosity about the world, especially a region that had become a theater of the Cold War, that had brought him and Lurine to Vienna. But there was another reason: They had learned that Ludwig Tröstler, a well-known luthier and owner of a prestigious violin shop in the city's center, had a fiddle to sell. Not just any fiddle but one painstakingly crafted in 1698 by Antonio Stradivarius. Named the Burmester after its early twentieth-century owner, the well-known German violinist Willy Burmester, the violin bore the personal stamp of Stradivarius, a Maltese cross framing the initials "A. S." It does not seem, however, to have borne the blood that trickled from Burmester's fingers while he practiced. The violinist claimed that he sold the violin because he could no longer play it. Relentless rehearsing, he said, had ravaged the skin and nerves on his fingertips.[4]

In one of the many famous lines from *The Third Man*, a Viennese black marketeer remarks, "I've done things that would have seemed unthinkable before the war." Jacob might well have uttered the very same words, though for utterly different reasons, when Tröstler handed over the reddish-brown spruce wood fiddle carved by Stradivarius two hundred and fifty years earlier. It was at that moment, one imagines, that he decided to buy it for $15,000. As a violinist, he was, of course, attuned to its unique musical qualities. When he cradled the fiddle under his chin and began to play, Jacob must have been struck by the celebrated "brightness" of the notes. (One recent scientific study suggests that the Strad is unique because its higher frequency tone resembles those made by female vocalists.[5]) As the child of an emigrant Jewish peddler who had worked the soil of North Dakota, Jacob was attuned to the equally unique qualities in his own life. The geographical, professional, and social distance he had traveled from his own beginnings in the Badlands to a violin shop in war-torn Vienna was breathtaking. The fabled brilliance of the Strads must have sounded even more brilliant in Jacob's ears as he fiddled on the Burmester.

Finally, as an entrepreneur with a keen eye for investments, Jacob grasped not just a few pounds of spruce wood but also its extraordinary market value. In this regard, Jacob was far-sighted. While Strads already promised a solid return on investment in the 1950s, their value skyrocketed in the decades that followed. The reasons for this trend, though, are somewhat elusive. For example, Strads are not especially rare. The Burmester that Jacob found in Vienna was one of slightly more than six hundred Strads in circulation. (In addition, there are also several dozen cellos and violas attributed to Stradivarius.) Moreover, it is not at all clear that the provenance—the most important indicator of a Strad's market value—of all these fiddles is dependable. For Laurence Libin, a former curator of musical instruments at the Metropolitan Museum of Art, the sheer number of extant Strads makes him doubt that all of them, in fact, were made by Stradivarius.[6]

Nevertheless, with a yearly appreciation rate of 8 percent, Strads offer a high and seemingly invincible return on investment. Along with the accruing of financial capital, they also lend themselves to the amassing of social capital. For a host of reasons, few that have to do with their actual sound, Stradivari fiddles have been the defining measure of social cachet no less than financial value. Even if you cannot distinguish between the timber of an Amati and a Strad, the odds are that your eyes will bulge only on hearing the latter's name. Some soloists, insists the violin dealer Rene Morel, pretend to play a Stradivari even when they're not. Why? "Because they know that audiences and critics expect them to. Such is the violin's mystique."[7]

In a sense, the value of a Stradivarius is arbitrary. Like tulips in mid-seventeenth-century Holland or Cabbage Patch Kids in late-twentieth-century America, Strads are sought after because they are sought after. Of course, unlike tulips or stuffed toys, they make glorious sounds. But does this sound justify their astronomical cost? Interestingly, once Jacob purchased the Burmester from Tröstler and brought it home, he did not often play it. If his fingers did not do what he wanted them to do on the hand-me-down violin he had in St. Paul, Jacob must have been even more sensitive to the gap between his own musical ability and the instrument's notoriety. Not only did he play the Strad rarely, Joyce recalls, but when he did, it was usually in the privacy of his office.

In 1978, Jacob decided to part ways with the Burmester. If he did regard the violin primarily as an investment, the time seemed ripe to play it for what it was worth. It turns out it was worth $100,000 (which translates into more than $460,000 in current value). For the sale, Jacob had employed the services of the French-born and New York–based violin dealer Jacques Français. He ranked among the most influential dealers during the last decades of the century, negotiating the sale of roughly half a dozen Stradivarius and Guarnerius del Gesu violins every year—a number estimated to be as many as half the world sales.[8] When Jacob learned from Français that he had struck the deal for the Burmester, he replied that though he was gladdened by the news, he was also saddened to part with it.[9]

But Jacob had not heard the last of the Burmester. The sale negotiated by Français had been with National Iranian Radio and Television (NIRT), a government agency that oversaw cultural programming under the Shah of Iran. A year after the sale was completed, the revolution in Iran brought an end to the Shah's rule. In the confusion and chaos that marked those early days, the Burmester disappeared from its location at NIRT. Three years later, in 1982, it resurfaced at a Sotheby's auction in New York City. Upon learning of the upcoming sale, the regime of Ayatollah Khomeini sued for the violin's return, claiming it had been stolen by an Iranian businessman, N. Z. Behroozian, who had fled the country with it. Fearing for his life, Behroozian at first refused to appear in federal court, just the first of many obstacles that litter the course of this peculiar case. In 1987, the court finally found in Behroozian's favor, ending what one of the lawyers called "a tale straight out of Ali Baba."[10]

More than a quarter-century had passed between the purchase and sale of the Burmester. It was an extraordinarily eventful period in Jacob's life, laced with great triumphs and great tragedies. Two years after Jacob and Lurine's son Philip was diagnosed with Hodgkin's disease—a period during which he underwent treatment at the Mayo Center in Minnesota—the young man died on February 16, 1965. A globe-trotter like his father, Philip had embarked on a promising career in engineering upon his graduation from the University of Oklahoma. Unlike his father, though, Philip also raced cars as a pastime. Several years later, Jacob recalled how he worried about his son's hobby. "I used to tell him: 'Philip, I'm going to get a call one night telling me you've cracked up in a car and you're dead.'" After a slight pause, Jacob added, "It didn't happen that way."[11]

Shortly before his death, Philip moved to Houston for medical care at the Texas Medical Center. With Philip's death, the bereaved parents decided to remain in Houston. Perhaps by way of distraction, Jacob and Lurine threw themselves into art collecting. This pastime, which soon became a passion, had begun years earlier in Oklahoma City. From their travels in the 1950s, the Greenbergs would bring home a rich and eclectic mix of art and antiques, ranging from pre-Columbian Peruvian and ancient Tibetan statues through illuminated medieval manuscripts from Europe to an early nineteenth-century Russian desk carved from Karelian birch and ancient Coptic textiles.

During this decade, they also acquired their first major painting, a winter street scene in Montmartre, by Maurice Utrillo. The Greenbergs had purchased the painting in 1952, three years before Utrillo's death. By then, the painter's critical reputation had begun to decline, perhaps from overexposure to his works being mass-produced on the very same medium—postcards—that he painted from during much of his life. Moreover, Utrillo's sheer productivity during the first half of the twentieth century, as well as the relative ease with which his style could be copied by hack artists, also dampened critical enthusiasm. (It is worth noting that Utrillo, calmed with wine as a child, struggled his entire life with alcoholism. His mother, Suzanne Valadon, a trapeze artist who became a remarkable pictorial artist in her own right, encouraged him to paint as a substitute for drinking. At first, the therapy worked, but its effect soon waned. Later in life, Utrillo often painted for his drinks, making him even more productive than he might otherwise have been.[12])

Yet, the appeal of Utrillo's paintings, with their chalky-white renderings of his native Montmartre—the outlying village of Paris that the city had annexed in the mid-nineteenth century—was deep and abiding for a generation whose own world was changing so rapidly and dramatically. (A world increasingly defined by an aesthetic, like the Googie style that shaped Jacob's bowling alley, that does not bother to look back.) As a result, the mid-twentieth century saw a thriving market in nostalgia, a fascination with the way we were. Or, more often, the way we never were but wish we had been, epitomized by the 1951 classic *An American in Paris*, in which Vincente Minelli, the director, transforms Montmartre into a dreamscape for the American middle class.

While the Utrillo canvas was Jacob and Lurine's first acquisition, it remains—along with a second Utrillo, a gouache and graphite painting of a chateau—an outlier in their collection. Far from paintings that convey a nostalgic longing for the past, the Greenbergs were instead drawn to German expressionism, which (aptly) expressed a radical critique and brutal rupture with the past. Expressionist artists fall, a bit too neatly, into one of two schools or movements: Die Brücke (the Bridge), founded in Dresden (though it soon moved to Berlin), and Der Blaue Reiter (the Blue Rider), based in Munich. Their differences were overshadowed by their similarities, yet those similarities are difficult to describe. Less a movement with clearly defined traits than a shared (and often dark) mood, expressionist painters, many of them with little or no formal training, used fierce colors, distorted forms, and blunt brushstrokes in their work. They presented a jarring contrast to French impressionism, whose practitioners remained on the surface of nature, fascinated by the play and perception of light. German expressionists instead plunged below the surface, absorbed by questions of human nature and self-perception.

Nearly all the expressionist artists in the Greenberg collection—ranging from Emil Nolde and Max Pechstein to Erich Heckel and Karl Schmidt-Rottluff—belonged to Die Brücke at one time or another. Often, however, this shared membership failed, ironically, to bridge the political and personal differences among these artists. By the time Nolde joined the group in 1906, he had already established his reputation as one of Germany's most influential artists. In his memoir, he wrote that he painted "the way I think it should be done."[13] Unhappily, he also practiced politics the way he thought it should be done. In 1933, Nolde enthusiastically welcomed the Nazi rise to power and praised Adolf Hitler as "great and noble in his aspirations and a genius of action." He broadcast his enthusiasm by flying a Nazi banner over his house and joining the NSDAP in 1934. Not surprisingly, he was also anti-Semitic, a hatred that, as the historian Michael Kater suggests, may have resulted from Nolde's artistic quarrel with the German-Jewish painter Max Liebermann and his eventual exclusion from the Berlin Secession movement. The Reich propaganda minister Joseph Goebbels, who had declared that expressionism conveyed the depths of the German soul, even hung several Nolde canvases in his home.[14]

They did not remain hung for very long, though. Nolde's idol and Goebbels's boss was less than enthusiastic about expressionism. Hitler referred to Nolde as "that pig" and mocked expressionism as the "artistic stammering of charlatans." Hitler despised Nolde's use of biblical themes—oddly, a distaste shared by Liebermann—but also the "violent distortions and colors" in his paintings.[15] This jaw-dropping irony was compounded when, alongside the work of Liebermann and other German-Jewish artists, Nolde's paintings were displayed at the Degenerate Art exhibition in 1937. After the war, Nolde skillfully reinvented his relationship with the Nazi regime. He recast the requirement to seek authorization to sell new paintings into an outright ban to paint, naming the hundreds of watercolors he created during this period—including the dazzling examples in the Greenberg collection—as "unpainted pictures." Nolde thus portrayed himself as a victim of the Nazis, hounded and harassed for his refusal to paint as they wished. This self-reinvention was so skillful that it was not until 2016 that the work of researchers compelled the Nolde Foundation to acknowledge that their patron was not a persecuted hero, but a failed collaborator.[16]

The relationship between Nolde and Pechstein, one of Die Brücke's founders, veered from mutual admiration to mutual distrust. In 1905, Pechstein and Heckel, overwhelmed by the "storms of color" they experienced at a Nolde exhibit, had invited the much older artist to join their movement. Just a few years later, though, the two men faced off as candidates for the leadership of the New Secessionist movement, a race that Pechstein lost to the more established Nolde. These tensions exploded soon after the Nazi rise in 1934. To ingratiate himself with the new regime, Nolde denounced Pechstein as a Jew in 1934 to Goebbels's Reich Propaganda Ministry. Not only did the denunciation threaten his professional existence, but as the "Aryan" Pechstein told Nolde, it was simply false. When Pechstein demanded that Nolde correct his mistake, however, the latter refused, declaring that he was "entirely disinterested" in Pechstein's fears over his livelihood.[17]

As a professional artist, Pechstein found himself in an impossible position during the 1930s: He was shunned in the US as a German and spurned in Germany as a Jew. Unlike some of his fellow expressionists like Ernst Ludwig Kirchner,

Pechstein never harbored anti-Semitic sentiments. He found the distinction between Aryan and Jew to be specious: "For me the decisive thing is the human being as such, and I will not be robbed of my Jewish friends who are reliable and kind."[18] One of the paintings in the Greenberg collection, his dazzling portrait of his first wife Charlotte "Lotte" Kaprolat, dates from one of Pechstein's most productive periods, 1919–1921. The daughter of working-class parents, Lotte was sixteen when she met Pechstein. She became his favorite model and, upon turning eighteen two years later, Pechstein married her.

A wispy watercolor of a nude, dating from 1924, also adorns the collection. A third painting, a dark oil scene of docked boats in a harbor in the Pomeranian town of Leba, probably also dates from 1919–1921, when Pechstein first discovered this bucolic retreat. There is also a late pencil and charcoal drawing of two boats made in 1949, the only one that dates from the postwar period. Though Pechstein had emerged from the war as one of Germany's most celebrated (and least compromised) painters, his influence with younger artists had largely waned. His influence was further diluted by new geo-political realities: In 1949, as well, Germany was formally divided between the communist eastern and democratic western halves. Keenly aware that expressionism and Soviet social realism did not mix, Pechstein remained in West Germany until his death in 1955.

The collection bristles with other German expressionists, along with several paintings by the Frenchman Georges Rouault, a prolific artist whose religious preoccupations, exaggerated figures, and rich colors all reflect expressionist traits. But expressionism does not exhaust the collection's holdings.

There are notable works by Otto Dix and Käthe Kollwitz. A towering figure of the postwar Neue Sachlichkeit, or New Objectivity movement, Dix's savagely satiric paintings blasted the political, industrial, financial, and military elites that had butchered German soldiers during World War I and beggared the survivors during the subsequent years of hyperinflation and depression. How different, though, is the late Dix work in the Greenberg collection—a watercolor of a loose knot of flowers executed in warm green and yellow colors.

Though not part of the New Objectivity movement, Kollwitz shared its sense of moral outrage over the material and social ills that afflicted the poor. She always believed that art must serve others. "I felt that I have no right to withdraw from the responsibility of being an advocate. It is my duty to voice the sufferings of human beings, the never-ending heaped mountains high." As for those who insisted upon the ideal of art for art's sake, Kollwitz had little patience. "One can say a thousand times that it is not pure art because it includes a purpose, but I want to be effective with my art as long as I can."[19] Kollwitz's deep moral imperative courses through two prints in the Greenberg Collection: *The Beggars* and *The Prisoners*. The former is a devastating lithograph from 1924 depicting a small group of children, their eyes as wide as the empty bowls raised above their heads. Drawn for a poster declaring "Germany's Children Are Hungry!" it has since been frequently adopted for humanitarian causes. The latter dates from 1908, the last of seven etchings that form the famous series *The Peasants' War*. Commissioned by the Society for Historical Art, the etchings were inspired by the sixteenth-century rebellion of German peasants. The rebellion's violence was far outstripped by its suppression—a moment that Kollwitz captures in her depiction of peasants waiting for their execution. Perhaps most striking, though, is a charcoal-on-paper self-portrait. Done late in life, after what she called the "outbreak" of Nazism in Germany, Kollwitz portrays herself with her head slightly bowed; her hair pulled tight behind her ears with a few stray hairs floating above her lined brow. With her right arm braced across her chest, her hand cradles her chin. Kollwitz's face is worn and tired, but her expression is absorbed yet attentive. It is an expression of someone who, having experienced the horrors of total war and totalitarianism, has not resigned herself to either one or the other.

As devastated as his wife by their son's death, Jacob also threw himself more deeply into work. In fact, even before Philip's untimely death, Jacob had already launched himself into new lines of business in Houston, both as vice president of Atlas-Bradford, an oil field supplies company, as well as the secretary-treasurer of a seismic analysis outfit, Seismic Computing Corporation.

In 1966, Jacob took on a third, and even larger, corporate challenge when he and a group of investors made a bid for control of the Chattanooga Gas Company. After a proxy legal battle against a competitor, Tennessee Natural Gas Lines, the court decided in Jacob's favor. With this victory, Jacob's group wrested 50 percent representation on the company's board of directors, and Jacob was named the company's president.[20]

At first glance, it seems nearly perverse to assume control of a natural gas company in the heart of a region shaped by the Tennessee Valley Authority. Yet Jacob, recalling the lessons he learned in economic geography, had done his homework. In an interview with the *Chattanooga Times*—a paper owned and operated by the *New York Times*—Jacob carefully explained the many factors that made Chattanooga, though located in the electrified backyard of the Tennessee Valley Authority, a natural for natural gas. He listed its school and park systems, its diversified industrial base, and its regional role as a transportation hub. No less important, he adds, were the residents: "An intelligent, literate, and industrious working population which is matched by a vigorous group of businessmen."[21]

A savvy salesman, Jacob never missed the chance to remind potential customers of the chance natural gas offered them. It was not just good for the local economy, he declared, but also for its ecology. In another interview published in the *Chattanooga Times,* for example, he observed, "We now hear about air pollution and water pollution. Whole populations have suddenly realized that the burning of natural gas for homes and industry is a ready-made solution to a great share of these problems."[22] In later interviews and articles, Jacob continued to boast of the environmental advantages afforded by natural gas. Thanks to its "efficiency, low pollution, and minimum environmental impact," Jacob declared that natural gas was the "wonder fuel of the century."[23] (Of course, by the end of that century, such claims were, at best, controversial. The inconvenient truth is that methane, which is released during the production process for natural gas, is 120 times more powerful than CO2 at trapping heat.)

Among the local movers and shakers Jacob had won over was Martin Ochs, the editor of the *Chattanooga Times.* In a long and admiring profile, Ochs described the director of the Chattanooga Gas Company in 1968 as "able, shrewd, and forceful. He has a lot of moxie and is a pretty good psychologist, too."

As CEO of Chattanooga Gas Company, Jacob Greenberg oversaw the expansion of the company's pipe network

Though he described himself as an "inveterate TVA addict"—the Tennessee Valley Authority had, after all, transformed the economic and social landscape of the American South—Ochs acknowledged the importance of alternate sources of energy like natural gas. As a booster for the local economy, Ochs also emphasized the sharp increases in the company's operating revenues and stock value; it was one of only two local companies then listed on the American Stock Exchange.[24]

Local papers were not alone in their praise of Jacob's economic and civic contributions to Chattanooga. In 1970, Jean Monaghan, a staff writer for the *Investment Dealers' Digest*, described the Chattanooga Gas Company as a "David in Goliath country." Since Jacob assumed control of the company five years earlier, Monaghan noted, his "management and merchandising have nearly doubled the volume of natural gas sold and boosted per-share earnings from fifty-eight cents to one dollar and forty-two cents."[25] For better or worse, she used the word *shrewd*, as did Ochs, to describe Jacob's management style, which included the introduction of "radio-controlled trucks to speed service" and offering more reliable estimates for its rates. But Jacob's impact went deeper than merchandising innovations. The company made dramatic investments in its infrastructure, plowing more than $16 million into the building of new pipelines across the city and environs.

By 1971, shortly after Chattanooga Gas merged with the Chicago-based energy company Jupiter Industries, Jacob announced that the company would make an even more significant investment: the construction of a liquified gas plant in Chattanooga. In an address to the city's business leaders, Jacob explained why his company had decided to assume the projected $9 million cost. "The Chattanooga Gas Co. is a public utility and, as such, we have a public trust. We are conscious every day of our obligation to our customers, and from a practical point of view we know that in the long run we cannot prosper unless we enlarge the reservoir of community good will we now enjoy." Not surprisingly, Jacob's commitment to the city's future was welcomed by Hammond Fowler, the chairman of the Tennessee Public Service Commission. "It is a source of gratification," he assured Jacob at the same event, "that your gas company feels justified in making the tremendous investment for the years ahead."[26]

Against the backdrop of the invasion of Israel by a coalition of Arab states in October 1973, the so-called Yom Kippur War, and the oil crisis caused by the subsequent oil embargo from Middle East producers, the recent completion of the plant seemed prescient. In an opinion piece for the *Chattanooga Free Press*, Jacob reassured readers that thanks to its long-term contract, his company would continue to fulfill its obligations to its customers. At the same time, though, Jacob argued that the government had to change its regulatory policies to encourage drilling in the United States. "The plain unvarnished truth is that we are really faced with an energy crisis within the next five or six years. The situation is far worse than most people realize."[27]

While Jacob's fears proved accurate, his hopes to play a role in meeting the crisis were soon dashed. In April 1974, Jacob learned the Federal Power Commission had ordered Chattanooga Gas Company's natural gas plant to "cease operations." Despite the temporary approval it had granted two years earlier, the FPC had now concluded that the plant had been built too close to neighboring houses. Whereas self-containment dikes had to be at least 400 feet from residential lines, the existing dikes of the Chattanooga plant were at times as close as 114 feet to private property.[28]

The FPC's decision was as shocking as it was surprising. In an official statement, Jacob declared that he was "dumbfounded" by the news. His astonishment appears justified. Not only was the plant's construction supervised by the Transportation Department's Office of Pipeline Safety, but the plant also met all relevant federal safety requirements and those applied by city, county, and state agencies. In a motion to reconsider the FPC's decision, Chattanooga Gas included an official letter from Joseph Caldwell, the director of the Office of Pipeline Safety, stating that the plant had been constructed in "full compliance with the codes, and it represents no hazard to life or adjoining property." In a registered letter he sent on April 24, Jacob reassured Gerald Wexler, the president of Jupiter Industries, that Caldwell's document "will, no doubt, reverse [the FPC's] opinion and Chattanooga Gas will be in the clear."

Despite Jacob's optimism, the FPC did not reverse its initial decision. Instead, in a settlement proposal, it maintained the cessation order until the company undertook the necessary steps to address several problems, including the installation of an alarm system and the construction of a sump to contain leakage from the plant's storage plants. Chattanooga Gas satisfied the requirements in less than a month, and on June 24, 1974, the commission allowed it to resume full operations. Tellingly, two dissenting commissioners made clear their opposition to the original order. Chattanooga Gas, one of them declared, "had absolutely no choice but to cave to this . . . pathetic case of bureaucratic abuse of statutory authority." Yet, one imagines that the local residents whose properties abutted the plant were relieved, not outraged, by this instance of bureaucratic abuse.[29]

By the time the cessation order was lifted, however, Jacob had ended his relationship with the company. On June 1, the *Chattanooga Free Press* announced Jacob's resignation from his position as president.[30] While he agreed to remain during the transition period, the letters exchanged between Jacob and Edward Ross, the president of Jupiter, were terse. The latter merely thanked Jacob for his "past services," while the former reminded Ross that full compensation had been agreed upon through May and not April, as Ross implied. Rather than ending with even perfunctory thanks, Jacob concluded with the assurance of his "full cooperation" with the transition.[31]

What had happened? It is difficult to know with certainty. The *Free Press* had reported that "Mr. Greenberg did not elaborate on his announcement."[32] Years later, Jacob told Joyce that he had resigned out of frustration. While the source of his frustration remains unclear, it may have been Jupiter's failure to fully support Jacob when the FPC order landed with a thud on the company's desk. Or the frustration may have been that of a man of professional accomplishments who, having just turned seventy, decided to turn his attention to personal matters.

Undoubtedly, Lurine was the most important of these matters. Her health seems to have long been frail, but it was only when Lurine and Jacob flew to Amsterdam in the spring of 1975 that they discovered how frail. The plane had scarcely touched the ground when Lurine told Jacob that she felt a great weight on her heart. Rather than seek medical attention in a foreign city, the Greenbergs decided to abort their trip and return immediately to Houston. Upon landing, Lurine was sped to Methodist Hospital for emergency surgery, but she died from complications on the operating table. Overwhelmed by grief over his wife's death and anger over what he believed was the emergency team's failure, Jacob found himself without the life partner he had known and loved for nearly a half-century. Shortly after her funeral, his life unsettled and future uncertain, Jacob left Houston to spend several months touring Africa.

The news of Lurine's death shocked Joyce Zeger Kaplan. A stockbroker at the Houston investment firm of Cowen and Co., Joyce had met Lurine at the Houston chapter of the League of Women Voters. Since 1971, she was also one of Jacob's several financial advisors. As Jacob tended to dispense rather than seek advice, Joyce's position required both a good deal of tact and a sure grasp of facts. With an abundance of both, Joyce had become a trusted sounding board for Jacob, who, since his departure from Chattanooga Gas, gave particular attention to his investment portfolio.

In 1969, when Joyce became a stockbroker, she also became a trailblazer. Women who worked in stock brokerages and investment banks in that era almost always did so as secretaries. Not surprisingly, when Joyce applied for a position as a stockbroker at the Houston office of Merrill Lynch, she received an offer of a secretarial position in return. Angered by the response, Joyce refused to accept the offer. Instead, she applied to a smaller firm, Rowes Winston, which had the wisdom to hire her as one of their stockbrokers. Shy and introverted, she found the experience of cold calling "miserable," but she persisted and worked her way up the ladder of stockbrokers. Shortly after she was hired at Rowes Winston, the firm was bought out by Cowen and Co., which no less wisely kept on Joyce. (It was with Cowen and Co. that Joyce, unaware that Lurine was married to Jacob, cold-called on him at his office. At first, he treated Joyce as he did all stockbrokers looking for his business: He showed her politely but firmly to his door. It was only later that he would pass by her office, across the street from his own, on most afternoons to talk shop and, he insisted, enjoy the free coffee.)

A single mother to two young daughters, Joyce had become a stockbroker out of necessity, not desire. In 1969, she divorced her husband and had to make her own way in a world dominated by men. Joyce showed a degree of will and grit that, oddly, still surprises her. Born in New York City in 1932, Joyce faced daunting challenges. Her mother, Beatrice Leichner Zeger, suffered from severe bipolar disorder. In an era before the discovery of lithium, the disorder was treated with barbiturates, a treatment often more debilitating, even more deadly, than the disease itself. Among the many side effects is addiction—it is estimated that more than a quarter of a million Americans were addicted to barbiturates in the 1950s—confusion, migraines, and sedation. This last side effect explains why Joyce remembers her mother sleeping during the day and awake—fiercely awake—during the night. Tragically, it also explains her mother's suicide in 1958.

It also explains the next stage in her life. As with Jacob, Joyce also graduated from one of the country's most prestigious schools. In her case, the University of Chicago, which she entered in the middle of her junior year of high school in New Jersey. The decision was made not by Joyce, however, but by her father, Baruch Zeger, whose family had emigrated from Lithuania. Learning from a colleague about Chicago's remarkable BA program for high school students, Zeger concluded, without consulting Joyce, that his daughter would go there. (While he was aware of Chicago's reputation, he was less aware that there was a highly selective application process.)

Less from a keen desire to attend Chicago than a keen need to escape her mother, the diffident sixteen-year-old agreed to apply. Several weeks later, Joyce was surprised to learn that she was accepted. With a mixture of anxiety and excitement, she began her studies at Chicago in the fall of 1948. Though she found her fellow students "brilliant and intimidating," Joyce overcame the social and emotional challenges confronting a teenager raised by a volatile mother and distracted father. She still speaks with great pride of being a "Hutchins girl," the moniker given to the young women who attended Chicago during the transformative and enlightened leadership of its president, Robert Hutchins. (Joyce recalls that her fellow classmates would pile every morning into her dorm room, whose window faced Hutchins's official residence. They all stretched their heads to watch the tall and handsome president taking his young stepdaughter's hand as they stepped out of the house and walked to her school.)

Joyce Zeger (on the right), posing with her friend Irvina Perman Warren, at their graduation from the University of Chicago

Upon her graduation in 1952, Joyce returned to her home in Passaic, New Jersey. Since her departure, the atmosphere had grown heavier and her mother more erratic than when she had left for school four years earlier. Eager to escape the house, Joyce found a job at the fashionable B. Altman department store, a short block from the Empire State Building in New York City, where she was assigned to the store's famous "flying squads," which were dispatched to departments overwhelmed by a sudden influx of customers. Like Jacob, however, Joyce soon found her way to garments when she moved from B. Altman after one year to the city's flagship Bloomingdale's department store, selling young girls' clothing. After one year, however, Joyce left Bloomingdale's—she did not agree with the findings of her annual review—and became a buyer for "better dresses" at Kirby, Block and Company, located in the city's famous garment district. Joyce's stint at Kirby, Block ended in 1956 when she married William Kaplan. The union, heavy with discontent and disappointment, produced her daughters Judith and Barbara but little else. Nevertheless, it lasted until 1969, when Joyce filed for divorce and found herself preparing for a career as a stockbroker.

Yet, it was this career that eventually led Joyce's path to cross Jacob Greenberg's. Though the initial meeting in 1971 was inauspicious, Jacob hired Joyce a few days later as one of his brokers. The business relationship between Mrs. Kaplan and Mr. Greenberg stretched over the next several years. Two years after Lurine's death, however, the relationship changed dramatically. After their third date in 1977, when they went to a screening of the film *The Red Shoes*, Jacob proposed to Joyce in the tearoom at the old Sheraton Hotel in Houston. Jacob's proposal was oddly indirect, however. He informed Joyce he was leaving town to see his daughter Abby. Gazing at Joyce, he explained that it was to ask her daughter's permission to remarry. A long moment passed before Joyce realized, with great joy, that Jacob wished to marry her.

The seventeen years of marriage that followed teemed with cultural and philanthropic activities. They made many foreign trips during these years—a tradition stretching back to Jacob's travels with Lurine and even his graduate studies in economic geography. But these visits also reflected, under Joyce's gentle influence, a new turn toward historic preservation. In the early 1990s, the Greenbergs enlisted in a remarkable project, the Jewish Heritage Program, undertaken by the World Monuments Fund. Launched in 1988, the program seeks to protect Jewish sites across the world threatened by either conflict or carelessness. Among the sixty sites they have either fully restored or are in the process of restoring is the Tempel Synagogue in Kraców, Poland. Built in 1862 and a splendid mingling of Moorish and neo-Romanesque influences, the synagogue is notable not just for its design but also its function: Located in one of the most ancient Jewish communities in Europe, it housed a Reform Jewish congregation. Thanks, in part, to a sizable donation from the Greenbergs, the fully restored synagogue has reopened for religious services and cultural events. Several other cultural organizations, including the Houston Grand Opera and the Society for the Performing Arts, are numbered among many charities supported by Jacob and Joyce. Notably, there is also the fund he began in Lurine's name with the Houston Public Library Fine Arts Trust. (Managed by Joyce since 1980, the Lurine Greenberg Fund has channeled more than $2 million into the library's trust.)

Most notable, however, were the trips that Joyce and Jacob made within the United States. It was at Joyce's urging that she and Jacob visited the North Dakota homestead where he was born. The first time Jacob had stepped foot on Badlands soil since he moved to St. Paul while still a toddler, he and Joyce spent days in the local archives researching the family's history. No less importantly, Joyce played a pivotal role in reaffirming the ties between Jacob and the remaining members of the Greenberg clan with whom he had lost contact. "One of the best things that Jacob did for our family," observed his nephew Donald Rossoff, "was to bring Joyce into our world."

Rossoff spoke those words in 1995 in his official capacity as a rabbi to mark the death and honor the life of Jacob Greenberg. In his eulogy, he recalled the presence of Jacob and Joyce at his rabbinical ordination in 1981, just as he recalled that "Uncle Jacob got into some intense discussions with some of my professors." But, he noted, that was his uncle. "All in all, Jacob was not a complicated man," Rossoff declared in his eulogy. "What you saw was what you got. He was a man who knew who he was, who had his own perspective on life forged out of his training, his experience in the world, his values and his passions. Jacob played no games, he curried no

Jacob and Joyce Z. Greenberg

favor; he called it like he saw it. And yet, there was a compassionate side which we saw, a man who wanted to help people. Yes, in many ways he was his father, but in many ways, he was his mother as well, generous and supportive to those persons and institutions which he believed stood for something." Rabbi Rossoff, who had been raised by Jacob's older sister Nettie, then turned to Joyce: "Jacob shared his world with you and you, in turn, opened up worlds to him. . . . As blessed as I know you felt to have been married to him, I know that no man has ever had a more devoted and loving wife than he had in you. You brought life to his life."

A painting hanging in Joyce's apartment offers proof of these eloquent words. In 1949, several years before he bought the Utrillo painting of Montmartre, Jacob purchased an oil portrait of a bare-backed model by Moses Soyer. The painting, bathed in olive green and beige colors, reflects the ravishing traits found in the work of Soyer, who was, along with his twin brother Raphael, a leading member of the social realism movement. A group of painters who staked an enduring claim to the New York City art scene during the interwar years, the social realists not only portrayed the world naturalistically but also, not unlike Kollwitz, conveyed the harsh conditions of modern life through many of their paintings.

More than a half-century later, Joyce added several more Soyer paintings to the collection. While they are all striking, one stands out: Raphael Soyer's *Couple in Armchair.* Completed in 1935, the oil painting portrays a not-so-young couple in a brown armchair. Clad in a long-sleeve red top and checkered dress reaching just below her knees, crowned with a red bow struggling to corral her thick brown hair, the woman sits comfortably on the man's lap. While the left hand rests on his back and the other hand nestles on her lap, an elusive smile plays on her faint red lips while her eyes gaze toward an unseen object. Yet the man, wearing a brown jacket and white shirt, has eyes only for her, his hand resting easily on hers. He, too, is smiling. When asked to explain what drew her to this painting, Joyce replied, "It reminds me of home." The home, no doubt, that she never had as a child or young adult, but the home that she made with Jacob.

ENDNOTES

Chapter 1

1. Jonathan Raban, *Bad Land: An American Romance* (New York: Vintage, 1997), 8.
2. Kathleen Norris, *Dakota: A Spiritual Biography* (New York: Harper, 2001), 1.
3. John Klier, "Emigration Mania in Late Imperial Russia: Legend and Reality," in *Patterns of Emigration, 1850–1914*, ed. Aubrey Newman and Stephen Massil (London: Jewish Historical Society of England, 1996), 21–30.
4. Among the places where Am Olam colonies were established was New Jersey. See Deborah Popper, "Great Opportunities for the Many of Small Means: New Jersey's Agricultural Colonies," *Geographical Review* 96, no. 1 (January 2005): 24–49.
5. Sophie Trupin, *Dakota Diaspora: Memoirs of a Jewish Homesteader* (Lincoln: University of Nebraska Press, 1984), 28.
6. Eugen Weber, *Peasants into Frenchmen: The Modernization of Rural France, 1870–1914* (Stanford, CA: Stanford University Press, 1976), 5.
7. Quoted in Jack Glazier, *Dispersing the Ghetto: The Relocation of Jewish Immigrants across America* (Ithaca, NY: Cornell University Press, 1998), 8.
8. Jacob A. Riis, *How the Other Half Lives: Studies among the Tenements of New York* (New York: Scribner's, 1890), 105, 107–1.
9. Quoted in Glazier, *Dispersing the Ghetto*, 13.
10. Glazier, *Dispersing the Ghetto*, 31.
11. Riis, *How the Other Half Lives*, 105.
12. New York Institute of Technology and the Skyscraper Museum, *Housing Density: From Tenements to Towers*, published in conjunction with an exhibition of the same title at the Skyscraper Museum, New York, May 2019–March 2020, https://mcusercontent.com/d380da56947045b561f6b3ec1/files/a15b6843-bf25-4506-800f-f7ef7262ad55/Housing_Density_From_Tenements_to_Towers_The_Skyscraper_Musem.pdf.
13. Quoted in Glazier, *Dispersing the Ghetto*, 27.
14. Quoted by Taylor Spence, "Jeffersonian Jews: The Jewish Agrarian Diaspora and the Assimilative Power of the Western Land, 1882–1930," *Western Historical Quarterly* 41 (Autumn 2010): 327.
15. See Dominique Frischer, "Le baron Maurice de Hirsch et les juifs de Russie," *Archives juives* 44 (2011): 20.
16. Frischer, "Le baron Maurice de Hirsch," 24.
17. Quoted in Matthias Lehmann, *The Baron: Maurice de Hirsch and the Jewish Nineteenth Century* (Palo Alto, CA: Stanford University Press, 2022), 67.
18. Maurice de Hirsch, "My Views on Philanthropy," *North American Review* (July 1891): 2.
19. Lehmann, *The Baron*, 68.
20. Lehmann, *The Baron*, 11.
21. Glazier, *Dispersing the Ghetto*, 16.
22. Quoted in J. Sanford Rikoon, "Jewish Farm Settlements in America's Heartland," in *Rachel Calof's Story: Jewish Homesteader on the Northern Plains*, ed. J. Sanford Rikoon (Bloomington: Indiana University Press, 1995), 111.
23. Quoted in Tobias Brinkmann, "Between Vision and Reality: Reassessing Jewish Agricultural Projects in 19th Century America," *Jewish History*, 21 (2007): 317.
24. Rikoon, "Jewish Farm Settlements," 114.
25. Rikoon, 112.
26. Rikoon, 113.
27. Spence, "Jeffersonian Jews," 341.
28. Quoted in W. Gunther Plaut, *The Jews in Minnesota: The First Seventy-Five Years* (St. Paul, MN: American Jewish Historical Society, 1959), 101.
29. Plaut, *The Jews in Minnesota*, 67–68.
30. Rikoon, "Jewish Farm Settlements," 118.
31. William Sherman, "Prairie Mosaic: An Ethnic Atlas of Rural North Dakota," in *North Dakota Institute for Regional Studies* (Fargo, ND, 1983). See also "Historical Population Change Data (1910–2020)," United States Census Bureau, April 26, 2021, https://www.census.gov/data/tables/time-series/dec/pop-change-data-text.html.
32. Rikoon, "Jewish Farm Settlements," Introduction.
33. Richard Rowland, "Geographical Patterns of the Jewish Population in the Pale of Settlement of Late Nineteenth Century Russia," *Jewish Social Studies* 48 (Summer–Autumn 1986): 212.
34. Plaut, *The Jews in Minnesota*, 89.
35. Ross Boissoneau, "Traverse City's Jewish Community Holds a Sacred Gem," *Northern Express*, June 19, 2021, https://www.northernexpress.com/news/feature/traverse-citys-jewish-community-holds-a-sacred-gem/.

36. Receiver's receipt, October 1, 1887, Ramsey County Courthouse.
37. Nettie Greenberg Epstein to Devera Stocker, April 10, 1979, Jewish Historical Society of Michigan.
38. Norton Stern and William Kramer, "Central North Dakota's Jewish Farmers in 1903," *Western States Jewish Historical Quarterly* (1978): 4.
39. See Mary Cohen Ioannides, "Jewish Homesteader Memoir: A Woman's Story," in Leonard Greenspoon, *Jews and Gender* (W. Lafayette, IN: Purdue University Press, 2021), 125.
40. Rikoon, "Jewish Farm Settlements," 21–22.
41. Trupin, *Dakota Diaspora*, 28.
42. Rikoon, "Jewish Farm Settlements," 23.
43. Trupin, *Dakota Diaspora*, 28.
44. Trupin, 32.
45. Rikoon, "Jewish Farm Settlements," 24.
46. Rikoon, 17.
47. Rikoon, 22.
48. Trupin, *Dakota Diaspora*, 2.
49. Rikoon, "Jewish Farm Settlements," 125.
50. Rikoon, 62.

Chapter 2

1. Quoted in Rhoda Lewin, "Stereotype and Reality in the Jewish Immigrant Experience in Minneapolis," *Minnesota History* 46 (Fall 1979): 263.
2. W. Gunther Plaut, *The Jews in Minnesota. The First Seventy-Five Years* (St. Paul, MN: American Jewish Historical Society, 1959), 44.
3. Plaut, *The Jews in Minnesota*, 75.
4. Plaut, 117. Based on the active members of mostly Orthodox synagogues, these numbers are no doubt conservative.
5. Plaut, 71.
6. Plaut, 95.
7. Plaut, 188–189.
8. *Chattanooga Times*, September 20, 1971.
9. *Guide to Frogtown*, Ramsey County Historical Society archives.
10. John W. Larson, "'The Best School in the City,' Mechanic Arts High School: Its First 20 Years, 1896–1916," *Minnesota History* (Spring 2002): 5–6.
11. Larson, "'The Best School in the City,'" 9.
12. Plaut, *The Jews in Minnesota*, 211–212.
13. Plaut, 213.
14. John W. Larson, "Mechanic Arts High School: The Dietrich Lange Years, 1916–1939," *Minnesota History* (Summer 2006): 7.
15. Lisa Heinrich, "Remembering a Civil Rights Hero: Roy Wilkins in Minnesota," *Minnesota History* (Winter 2019–2020): 319.
16. Larson, "Mechanic Arts High School," 11.
17. John Higham, *Strangers in the Land: Patterns of American Nativism, 1860–1925* (New Brunswick, NJ: Rutgers University Press, 1988), 278.
18. Sophie Trupin, *Dakota Diaspora: Memoirs of a Jewish Homesteader* (Lincoln: University of Nebraska Press, 1984), 78.
19. Leonard Dinnerstein, "Anti-Semitism Exposed and Attacked, 1945–1950," *American Jewish History* (September 1981): 134.
20. Laura Weber, "Gentiles Preferred: Minneapolis Jews and Employment, 1920–1950," *Minnesota History* (Spring 1991): 170.
21. Weber, "Gentiles Preferred," 170.
22. Riv-Ellen Prell, "Anti-Semitism without Quotas at the University of Minnesota in the 1930s and 1940s," *American Jewish History* 105, nos. 1–2: 26.
23. Carey McWilliams, "Minneapolis: The Curious Twin," *Common Ground* (Autumn 1946): 61.
24. Plaut, *The Jews in Minnesota*, 271.
25. *A Campus Divided: Essays*, "Anti-Semitism at the University of Minnesota," University of Minnesota, 2017. Essay published in conjunction with a physical exhibit, *A Campus Divided: Progressives, Anticommunists, Racism, and Antisemitism at the University of Minnesota 1930–1942*, Andersen Library, University of Minnesota, August 14–December 22, 2017, https://acampusdivided.umn.edu/essay/antisemitism-at-university-of-minnesota/.
26. *A Campus Divided: Essays*, "Anti-Semitism at the University of Minnesota."
27. Hannah Arendt, *Eichmann in Jerusalem: A Report on the Banality of Evil* (New York: Viking Press, 1963).
28. Edmund Clingan, *The Lives of Hans Luther, 1879–1962: German Chancellor, Reichsbank President, and Hitler's Ambassador* (New York: Lexington Books, 2007), 132.
29. Clingan, *The Lives of Hans Luther*, 100.
30. Clingan, 100.
31. Clingan, 105.
32. Clingan, 104.
33. *A Campus Divided: Essays*, "Anti-Semitism at the University of Minnesota."
34. Prell, "Anti-Semitism without Quotas," 22.
35. "Jazz Band Is Featured," *Minnesota Daily*, October 9, 1924, https://conservancy.umn.edu/handle/11299/232681.

36. "Large Audience Applauds Music Seniors in Recital," *Minnesota Daily*, May 22, 1926, https://hdl.handle.net/11299/232953.

Chapter 3

1. Nathan Glazer, "The National Influence of Jewish New York," in *Capital of the American Century: The National and International Influence of New York City*, ed. Martin Shefter (New York: Russell Sage Foundation, 1993), 167.
2. 1925–1926 Directory of Students, Columbia University.
3. Columbia University School of Business Bulletin, 1924–1925.
4. Joyce Greenberg interview (February 27, 2023).
5. Ina Jaffe, "Yossele Rosenblatt: The Cantor with the Heavenly Voice," National Public Radio, September 6, 2010, https://www.npr.org/templates/story/story.php?storyId=129635330.
6. Quoted in Yair Rosenberg, "How Anti-Semitism Shaped the Ivy League as We Know It," *The Atlantic*, September 22, 2022, https://newsletters.theatlantic.com/deep-shtetl/632c8ea068f61f0021dbfd41/mark-oppenheimer-interview-jewish-ivy-league-antisemitism/.
7. Leeza Hirt, "Columbia for Jews? The Untold Story of Seth Low Junior College," *Current* (Fall 2016), http://www.columbia-current.org/seth_low_junior_college.html.
8. David Cohn, *The Good Old Days: A History of American Morals and Manners as Seen through the Sears Roebuck Catalogs 1905 to the Present* (New York: Simon and Schuster, 1940), xxx.
9. Peter Ascoli, *Julius Rosenwald: The Man Who Built Sears, Roebuck and Advanced the Cause of Black Education in the American South* (Bloomington: Indiana University Press, 1906), 31.
10. Quoted in Boris Emmet and John Jeuck, *Catalogues and Counters: A History of Sears Roebuck & Company* (Chicago: University of Chicago Press, 1950), 129–130.
11. Gordon Weil, *Sears, Roebuck, USA: The Great American Catalog Store and How It Grew* (New York: Stein and Day, 1977), 43.
12. Quoted in Ascoli, *Julius Rosenwald*, 37.
13. Quoted in Ascoli, 32.
14. Quoted in Cohn, *The Good Old Days*, 546.
15. Weil, *Sears, Roebuck, USA*, 52.
16. Quoted in Ascoli, *Julius Rosenwald*, 53.
17. Tobias Brinkmann, *Sundays at Sinai: A Jewish Congregation in Chicago* (Chicago: University of Chicago Press, 2012), 134–135.
18. Brinkmann, *Sundays at Sinai*, 230.
19. Weil, *Sears, Roebuck, USA*, 41.
20. Joyce Greenberg interview (February 27, 2023).
21. Emmet and Jeuck, *Catalogues and Counters*, 547–548.
22. So much more is unclear from this period due to my inability to get a response from the corporate archives at Sears. Coincidentally, Franz Kafka's novel *Das Schloss*, or *The Castle*, was published in Germany just one year before Jacob arrived in Chicago. The coincidence is apt: Reaching the Sears archives proved as impossible as the efforts of K., the novel's protagonist, to reach the castle that commanded him to come.
23. In an email dated March 1, 2023, the synagogue's executive director, Jan Kaufman, informed me that "we would not have these records available to us."
24. Joyce Greenberg interview (February 27, 2023).
25. Quoted in Emmet and Jeuck, *Catalogues and Counters*, 649.
26. Charles Lemons, *Uniforms of the US Ground Forces 1939–1945* (Lulu.com, 2012), 265

Chapter 4

1. Todd Purdum, "The 'Hamilton' of World War II," *New York Times*, March 31, 2018.
2. Andrea Most, "'We Know We Belong to the Land'": The Theatricality of Assimilation in Rodgers and Hammerstein's 'Oklahoma!'" *PMLA* 113 (January 1998): 82.
3. According to the 2010 census, the town boasted roughly 16,000 residents. In Linda D. Wilson, "Wewoka," in *The Encyclopedia of Oklahoma History and Culture*, The Oklahoma Historical Society, n.d., https://www.okhistory.org/publications/enc/entry.php?entry=WE023#:~:text=Wewoka%20was%20originally%20located%20in,before%20their%20removal%20from%20Florida.
4. Jewish Museum of the American West, "Early Jewish Pioneers of Chickasha, Oklahoma," 2021, https://www.jmaw.org/chickasha-jewish-oklahoma/.
5. Encyclopedia of Southern Jewish Communities, s.v. "Chickasha," accessed June 9, 2023, https://www.isjl.org/oklahoma-chickasha-encyclopedia.html. In 1994, the family sold the store, which has since become home for the Grady County Historical Museum.

6. *Chattanooga Times*, September 20, 1971.
7. Rachel Maines, "Wartime Allocation of Textile and Apparel Resources: Emergency Policy in the 20th Century," *Public Historian* 7 (Winter 1985): 34.
8. Library of Congress, "U.S. History Primary Source Timeline," accessed June 9, 2023, https://www.loc.gov/classroom-materials/united-states-history-primary-source-timeline/post-war-united-states-1945-1968/overview/
9. "Chaps," by Ralph Lauren [TV Commercial], YouTube, https://www.loc.gov/classroom-materials/united-states-history-primary-source-timeline/post-war-united-states-1945-1968/overview/
10. Tracey Panek, "The 80-Year Coverup," Levi Strauss & Co., July 6, 2017, https://www.levistrauss.com/2017/07/06/80-year-cover/.
11. Linda D. Wilson, "Wewoka."
12. *Wewoka Daily Times*, September 24, 1952.
13. Robert D. Parmet, *The Master of Seventh Avenue: David Dubinsky and the American Labor Movement* (NYU Press, 2005), 133, 261.
14. Benjamin Stulberg, *Tailor's Progress: The Story of a Famous Union and the Men Who Made It* (New York: Doubleday, 1944), 198–198.
15. Richard Greenwald, "'More Than a Strike': Politics, Legislation, and the IGLWU," *Business and Economic History* 27 (Winter 1998): 305.

Chapter 5

1. *Midcentury Marvels: Commercial Architecture of Phoenix, 1945–1975*, City of Phoenix Historic Preservation Office, n.d., 86.
2. Graham Greene, *The Third Man* (New York: Penguin, 1977), 24.
3. Brigitte Timmermann, *The Third Man's Vienna: Celebrating a Film Classic*, trans. Penny Black (London: European Schoolbooks, 2005), 68.
4. Phil McCombs, "Iran Files Suit to Reclaim Stradivarius Violin," *Washington Post,* December 1, 1982, https://www.washingtonpost.com/archive/lifestyle/1982/12/01/iran-files-suit-to-reclaim-stradivarius-violin/2a55c0a6-8f76-42cf-b0f2-9cb-51c3ac50d/.
5. Ian Sample, "Scientists Find Secret Behind Sweet Sound of Stradivarius Violins," *Guardian*, May 21, 2018, https://www.theguardian.com/science/2018/may/21/scientists-find-secret-behind-sweet-sound-of-stradivarius-violins.
6. Jon Gertner, "This Violin Is Worth $3.5 Million. Why?" *Money Magazine*, June 2002, 147.
7. Gertner, "This Violin is Worth $3.5 Million," 148.
8. Douglas Martin, "Jacques Français, 80, Dies; Dealer in String Instruments," *New York Times*, February 8, 2004.
9. Letter from Jacob Greenberg to Jacques Français, March 28, 1978.
10. James Rowley, "Rug Merchant Wins Possession of Stradivarius Violin from Iran," AP News, February 12, 1987, https://apnews.com/article/244534d7a035869873bf-66515708b8e0.
11. *Chattanooga Times*, September 20, 1971.
12. Jerrold Seigel, *Bohemian Paris* (New York: Penguin, 1987), 345.
13. Christian Ring and Hans-Joachim Throl, "An Artist's Life on the German-Danish Border," in *Emil Nolde: The Great Colour Wizard* (Berlin: Hirmer, 2015), 41.
14. Michael Kater, *Culture in Nazi Germany* (New Haven, CT: Yale University Press, 2019), 35.
15. Catherine Hickley, "Stripping Away Lies to Expose a Painter's Nazi Past," *New York Times*, April 10, 2019, https://www.nytimes.com/2019/04/10/arts/nolde-nazi-exhibition-berlin-merkel.html.
16. Bernhard Fulda and Aya Soika, *Max Pechstein: The Rise and Fall of Expressionism* (Berlin: De Gruyter, 2012), 302.
17. Fulda and Soika, *Max Pechstein*, 305.
18. Mina and Arthur Klein, *Käthe Kollwitz: Life in Art* (New York: Schocken Books, 1972), 83.
19. *Wall Street Journal*, February 2, 1966.
20. *Chattanooga Times*, November 16, 1966.
21. *Chattanooga Free Press*, September 10, 1971.
22. *Chattanooga Times*, December 19, 1968.
23. *Chattanooga Free Press,* June 8, 1969.
24. *Investment Dealers' Digest*, June 9, 1970.
25. *Chattanooga Free Press*, September 10, 1971.
26. *Chattanooga Free Press*, January 1, 1974.
27. *Wall Street Journal*, April 2, 1974.
28. United States Federal Power Commission, "Order Accepting Settlement Proposal," no. CP73-329, June 24, 1974.
29. Copy of a letter in Greenberg's personal papers.
30. *Chattanooga Free Press,* June 1, 1974.
31. Letters dated May 2 and May 3, 1974.
32. *Chattanooga Free Press,* June 1, 1974.